STRONG IN, STRONG OUT

The Dick Virgilio Story

Joe Ditler

For Beatrice, the love of my life.
Thank you for always being there for me.
This book is for you, our children, and our grandchildren.

Strong In, Strong Out: The Dick Virgilio Story

ISBN: 978-1-7320962-0-2
Printed in the United States of America

CONTENTS

FOREWORD

Today, just past my 80th birthday, it's easy for me to sit here in my favorite chair and look out over the water, reflecting on my life. My dog Skipper is at my feet. I'm not sure what he's reflecting on but he, too, looks content.

If you'd asked me about this a few years ago, I'd have scoffed at any suggestion of writing a book. After all, I never kept diaries or journals. I just lived as well as I could, taking care of those around me, those I loved; always trying to do the right thing.

For the past two years, Joe Ditler and I have sat here, tape recorder rolling, talking about everything under the sun. To my surprise, I was able to open up and share with him things that I hadn't even shared with my wife or children; things I hadn't thought about in decades.

I never felt my life was worthy of an article in the newspaper, much less a book. Yet, now that I have such a large family of children and grandchildren, it means a lot to me to leave a written legacy for them — to explain things they otherwise might not understand.

First of all, I thank the Lord for the day I met Bea, and for the birth of each of our five children and nine grandchildren. I am a very lucky and Blessed man. I've made my peace with the Lord, and when the time comes, I'll be ready.

My life has had no shortage of adventures, as you'll read as you turn the pages. The adventures continue, but now, as I write this, I'm comfortable and content in what will be my final home, here at the end of Point Loma, looking south and southwest across the water.

From my chair, I can look out over the channel to San Diego Bay, at the tip of Shelter Island, and the entrance to La Playa—also called the Gulch.

I love Fridays, when all the boats come into La Playa to anchor. They have 72 hours they can stay, so Monday morning they all leave.

Then, on Wednesday nights during the summer, we get to watch all the boats head out to the Beer Can races. They all sail right past my condo. There are the yacht club kids and their regattas. Last week they sailed the Dutch Shoe Marathon right past my front yard.

On a daily basis I see boat traffic—recreational and commercial. I see Harbor Police, Coast Guard, and Navy. I see all of the America's Cup charter sailboats.

Hardly a day goes by that I don't know somebody sailing out or in, or motoring out or in, or paddle boarding. I keep a couple of paddle boards and a kayak in the back and frequently Bea and I (and Skipper) will paddle down to the yacht club for morning coffee.

Everyone walks their dog out here in the front yard; we chat over coffee in the morning and wine in the evenings; people on the boats yell over, "Hey, Dick, how's it going?"

It's where I want to be. It's like being on a boat, but I'm at home. That's why I don't go down and use my boat much anymore. I have it all right here, out my front window. If I want privacy, I can just drop the blinds, but I seldom do.

We moved into our waterfront home in 1995 and, yeah, this is where we want to finish it all up. They'll have to drag me out of here feet first.

I hope those of you reading this book who encounter setbacks in life, be they medical or some other adversity, are inspired to never give up on fulfilling your dreams in life.

I did not let severe heart problems keep me from accomplishing my goals. I got tired of family, friends, and most of all my doctor peers, telling me that I couldn't do this or couldn't do that.

It would have been easy to have given up at any time along the way and become a couch potato. But I decided early on that, for me anyway, I would rather have a shorter life filled with memories of exciting family adventures and personal accomplishments than live out a boring life devoid of these elements.

To my friends who fear the future, I say, bury your fears and enjoy an active life for as long as you can. Don't feel sorry for yourself; actively interact with your loved ones, and give them memories they can cherish forever.

I hope all of you enjoy this book, and appreciate the often-embarrassing self-deprecation involved in reliving those moments. For those of you at a crossroads in life, you may relate to my story more than others.

I'd like to dedicate this book to all of my family and friends who played a role in making me the man I am today—the father and husband, the friend. In particular, I dedicate this to my good friend Nick Frazee, who passed on April 2, 2017, while this book was being written.

I was present when he passed, and I will always feel extremely fortunate to have had Nick as a friend. He was a loving husband, father, and a true friend to many of us in Point Loma. His devotion and loyalty to his family inspired us all to be better people. I think of him daily, and miss him dearly.

And, finally, I would like to thank Joe Ditler for his collaboration on this project. As I said, I entered into this mission with some trepidation. After my first session with Joe, instinct told me that he was indeed the right man to trust with my stories; the right man to trust with the raw emotion that would come with digging into a sometimes troubled past.

Joe listened with compassion and patience and wrote my story with humor, empathy, and attention to detail. His enthusiasm for the project buoyed me on more than one difficult occasion. Thank you, Joe, for your friendship and for your genius in bringing my story to these pages.

I hope you enjoy the book. God Bless you all.

Dick Virgilio
San Diego, California

INTRODUCTION

Welcome to the world of Dick Virgilio. Thank you for coming along with us on this ride—a journey that will make you laugh and make you cry.

Most of all, you'll shake your head in wonderment at how Dick managed to survive his early childhood in the brutal outskirts of Baltimore, with a mean and dysfunctional father, and a bullying brother.

His solution? Run away from home in the middle of the night and hitchhike across the country—to get as far away as his young mind could imagine.

In the years that followed, with the help of a loving mother and benevolent uncle, Dick began to carve out a new life, an education, and eventually a respected career and loving family of his own.

He worked in harsh and dangerous conditions as a surgeon in Vietnam, then returned home and created life-saving trauma care systems and procedures that changed the medical landscape throughout San Diego County forever.

Dick sailed singlehanded to Hawaii and explored the South Pacific, inspired by Jeff Chandler movies of his youth, and visions of Capt. Adam Troy in the old TV series, "Adventures In Paradise." He survived several heart attacks, three heart-bypass operations, and numerous other life-threatening heart incidents that would have finished a lesser man, but he never stopped chasing his dreams.

He is still amazed, at 80, that he has lived this long. Throughout the two years we spent researching and writing this book, his constant remark to me was, "Hurry up, Ditler. I don't know how much time I have left. I don't even buy green bananas these days."

The icing on the cake for Dick Virgilio was marrying Bea, the love of his life, and raising five children, who gave him nine grandchildren. His legacy, of course, is his family. But Dick Virgilio's long and winding path is one heck of a tale.

Yes, this is the story of a doctor, sailor, and family man. But what he had to overcome at every step of the way makes his tale more akin to a survival story, or a race to beat the clock.

But no, while I could go on and on about what a great man Dick Virgilio is, I'd prefer you to read for yourself in this, a book of his life, named for his motto in life: "Strong In, Strong Out."

I hope you enjoy reading Dick's story as much as I enjoyed retelling it. Even now, I could sit for hours at his knee, listening to him weave stories of his youth, or his sailing adventures, or about the people who influenced him throughout his long life.

Ladies and gentlemen? I give you Dr. Richard Virgilio . . .

— Joe Ditler
Coronado, California

ONE

A Childhood Worth Forgetting

The path of life is a strange one. Some are born to greatness; some are handed their success on a silver platter. Others fall by the roadside, often choosing the wrong signpost along the way, or neglecting to recognize opportunity when it comes knocking.

Then there are those who go through life pounding out their own destiny, flailing away at the roadblocks and distractions, blazing a trail through the wilderness of life.

And so it was for Richard William Virgilio, "Dick" to his family and friends.

In 1945, Dick was eight years old. He remembers coming out of a movie house and seeing people in the streets celebrating the end of the war. The Nazis had quit. An atomic bomb was let loose on Japan. The word "Peace" was in the headlines for the first time in a very long while. It was time to put the country back together. A time to heal.

Small town cinemas across the country were showing films to bolster American pride (and sell war bonds); these films, called "flicks" back then, included "Objective Burma," "G.I. Joe," and "They Were Expendable," "Going My Way," and "Double indemnity."

Big-band music filled the AM radio airwaves with tunes from such greats as Perry Como, Bing Crosby, Judy Garland, and Frank Sinatra.

Movies and music were the great healers both during and after World War II.

For a small boy living on the outskirts of Baltimore, none of this mattered. This was the home of Dick Virgilio, the seven-year-old son of Italian immigrants bent on getting into trouble at every opportunity; not caring whether he got caught. In fact, he hoped he would get caught, just so he could bring shame to his father.

Dick on the beach at Ocean City Maryland, Summer 1939.

Such was the mood in the Virgilio home. Like many families coming to America from the old country, love was not something that was spoken or openly displayed. In the Virgilio home, it proved to be a stake in the heart of their family.

Dick came into this world on December 11, 1937, the younger of two sons born to Rose Marino and Frank Virgilio . He lived on the outskirts of Baltimore with his mother, father, and older brother, Frank Junior.

The Virgilios never wanted for meals or a roof over their heads, but the patriarch of the family was an angry and malcontent man who generated that dark and gloomy tone wherever he went.

Their home was not a loving or embracing household. Frank Virgilio, Sr., had been described more than once as "a self-centered pain in the ass." In fairness, he accomplished much as an Italian immigrant.

He was proud to be an American. He wanted nothing to do with Italian gatherings and refused to speak his native language, except with his parents, who didn't speak English.

Frank's fatherhood skills consisted of an iron fist, a cold demeanor, and a raging temper. He seemed to have a chip permanently attached to his shoulder.

Dick's mother Rose was just the opposite. She taught school but gave that up to be a mother when her sons were born. She demonstrated her love through her cooking. She never sided with the children when they were in conflict with their father. She lived life in her husband's shadow – the old Italian way.

Frank Virgilio was a doctor and surgeon, a Columbia Medical School graduate who had come to Baltimore to do his internship and residency in surgery.

"It was a pretty good practice," recalled Dick, "until the Korean War broke out. My father was drafted into the navy and had to give up his practice."

* * *

Frank Senior had few friends. He got no respect from his peers. He treasured and pursued titles. He was, by his own accounting, the right and honorable Doctor, Captain Virgilio, sir—a man so lost in his own little world that it mattered not whether people liked him.

In Dick's words, "At best, people tolerated my father. And yet, in a social setting such as a cocktail party or dinner, people loved him, and he was the life of the party. He was a schmoozer when he thought it would get him somewhere. Then, as people got to know him better, that all changed."

"[He] never told me he loved me."

Childhood was not fun. In fact, it was so traumatic that, over the subsequent years of his life, he blocked large chunks of it completely out of his mind. Many years later, at the age of 79, he sat and struggled to remember pieces of that past. Yet, the more he spoke, the more memories came flooding back:

"My father was a very demanding man, so my mother spent most of her time caring for his needs, and mediating disputes between her sons and their father.

"There were no sports, no family trips or outings. My father never hugged me. He never played with me. In fact, I can't

Dick and brother Frank with paternal grandparents.

remember him ever showing any emotion or affection towards me whatsoever ... he never told me he loved me.

"He was a strict authoritarian. He seemed to live to make me feel I had been bad, or not worthy. He made me believe that I couldn't do anything right. Love and intimacy didn't exist within that man."

Fortunately for the youngest Virgilio, he would grow to become the antithesis of his father. He would be a loving husband and father, taking his kids on family outings—sailing trips, skiing trips, golfing; he was a man who never missed one of his children's sporting events.

It was with great difficulty that Dick had trouble dredging up those painful memories—an exercise he repeated the rest of his life.

He tried to reconcile with his father until his death—tried often to talk to him about these black holes in his childhood.

"When I was older, in my fifties, and after my mother died, I began to understand why my father had been so unloving to his children. I made a promise to myself that I would work hard at developing a meaningful relationship with him before he was gone forever. This promise became more and more difficult to keep as the years went on, but I was with him when he died. I knew within myself that I had kept my promise. I was finally at peace with myself."

Perhaps the ultimate blow came while he was preparing for college and wrote to his father to tell him he loved him. Dick was cursed with a terrible stutter in his youth and didn't discover until many years later he suffered from dyslexia. His father took the letter, marked in red ink every misspelled word or fragmented sentence, and mailed it back.

"That broke my heart," Dick later said of his father's act. "I never wrote to him again."

The effects of that returned letter haunted Dick for a long time. The question is, did it drive him or did it hold him back? In a way, it did both.

Dick spent a lifetime rationalizing his father's behavior.

"I look back on that and I realize my father's anger and behavior were probably just the Italian way, the way he was brought up, the way his father before him was brought up."

"I got in all kinds of trouble. My mother had to come to the school and get me. I was always looking to get into trouble in those days. If I went to steal an ice cream from the corner store, I was hoping I would get caught so my father would be humiliated. It was the only thing I knew I could do to hurt him. That was my mentality at the time."

His older brother, Frank, seemed to deliberately dislike Dick. While not that much older, Frank wouldn't play with his little brother, or even talk to him. In fact, the only interaction Dick remembers is that his brother knew Dick was ticklish, and took morbid delight in chasing him, catching him, holding him down, and tickling him until he cried, begged to his brother to stop, and the very breath left his lungs.

"My brother was two and a half years older. He never had any friends either. He never brought friends home, and it wasn't long before, like me, he wasn't even part of the family anymore."

Raised in such a loveless environment, with no encouragement or hope, it would be truly amazing to imagine Dick Virgilio somehow managing to leave that world, unfathomable that he would one day grow to be a groundbreaking trauma surgeon and raise a family of children and grandchildren with whom he had meaningful and loving relationships.

Dick Virgilio, in spite of (or because of) the negative reinforcement of his youth, grew to become a loving, communicating husband, father, and grandfather who couldn't get enough time with his family.

It was a miracle he survived those early days in Baltimore. And, as he would say years later, "I only knew one thing. I knew the type of father I did not want to be. I knew I didn't want to be my father."

* * *

The youngest of the Virgilio boys was built like a fireplug. He was a tough kid and didn't turn the other cheek for anyone. Even so, despite his troubled childhood, he wasn't what anyone would describe as a bully.

"I fought a lot of kids who were just like me. It seems as though I fought a lot, but I never picked on little kids or girls. And if I saw someone doing that, I would step in. When I did fight, I wasn't fighting a little wimp; I was fighting tough kids, like me—my size or bigger."

The kids he hung out with were a bit on the crazy side, he said. "We would do anything we could—steal things, break things." His "gang" consisted of three or four neighborhood kids and, in their own small way, they owned their outlying neighborhood of Baltimore—maybe

not the toughest neighborhood back then, but one to
be reckoned with.

"That was who I was
from the age of eight to
eleven. We just ran the
streets, climbing out the
windows at night, stealing
anything that wasn't tied
down. We loved to pull
pranks on people."

One of his favorite
tricks was to put dog crap
in a bag and set it on fire
on some poor guy's front
porch, then hide across
the street and watch as he
came out and stomped on
it in his stocking feet.

"I haven't thought
about that in years," he
said with a laugh. "Not
since I was a kid. And I
remember this big, heavy-
set lady, old lady Jessop I

Dick with brother Frank and mother Rose.

think her name was, who was a cashier in one of the many mom-and-
pop stores that dotted our neighborhood. We didn't have big super-
markets and the like, so we would distract her with something on the
inside, while another guy would steal fruit from the baskets outside.
Or, we would load up our pockets with bubble gum and then run like
hell.

"We just drove her crazy, and I don't know why we picked on her.

She had a little store we all hung out at and around. I moved away before she could see I grew up and changed my ways.

"If there was something to be done to cause trouble, we would figure out what it was. I can still remember her chasing me with a broom and the excitement I got knowing we had pulled it off."

It's funny how the memory plays tricks on a person. One day you can't remember a thing from your childhood. Then, the more you talk about it, the more that comes bubbling to the surface.

Such was the case with Dick Virgilio. As he sat years later in his favorite chair, he folded his hands behind his head, looked searchingly at the ceiling, and began to remember more and more from that childhood he had tried so hard to forget.

"There was always a local beat cop walking the streets," he said, looking amazed that this long forgotten memory had suddenly reared its head. "We would wait and hide until he walked by. We knew what time he was on, what time he went off, and what time he would walk by. We knew it all because that part of the city was our playground."

And girls? They didn't exist in the young Virgilio's life.

"I was very, very bashful. I didn't date at all in high school. I was afraid to ask a girl out. I was afraid to ask a girl to the school dance. I always felt I was ugly. I wasn't good looking, and I felt girls wouldn't want to go out with me. I guess I was afraid of getting rejected if I asked them to go somewhere or do something."

And yet, there was one girl he remembered clearly.

For the early part of his youth, Dick had a devastating stutter. It sapped his confidence and hurt his grades. Even his own father made fun of him.

"I never stuttered again after that."

"I finally got rid of that stutter. In first grade we would sit around in a semicircle and read from a book; each child in turn would read a page.

"When they came to me, my knees would shake, and I would

start stuttering. This went on for weeks, and this little girl in the group would always laugh at me. Then everyone else would start laughing, but I remember that she was the one who always started it.

"The teacher would tell her to stop, and explain that, 'Dick has a problem.' Then one day she was sitting right next to me in the reading circle. When she started to laugh, I just got up and whacked her one in the face. She went over her chair and landed on the ground. I never stuttered again after that," he said.

As the memories continued to flow, his face took on a look of disbelief, as though he couldn't imagine he was remembering all those long-ago details, much less that he actually did those things as a child.

"I wonder if she is still alive and sitting around with her own grandchildren, telling them about the day she got whacked in the face by a little boy for teasing him about his stutter."

Indeed, Dick Virgilio's childhood was confusing, forgettable, and one that somehow survived despite being beaten down constantly in a loveless household—the lowest man on the totem pole and clearly the easiest target.

The Baltimore Virgilios didn't go to baseball games, didn't go camping, didn't sit around the dinner table and talk about their day. It was a cold and lonely place that, in retrospect, seems like a holding station where people blindly pass through, then move on to other destinations. That's the way it was for Dick. And he has no warm thoughts of that time.

"People always talk about the wonderful things they did with their families as children. Not me. I know it's sad to say now, but we just never did things together as a family. While other people look back fondly on their childhoods and recite numerous memories of their parents and siblings, my childhood was a very forgettable time in my life."

Dick with his father and brother.

TWO

The Virgilio Home

Young Dick Virgilio had little to look forward to in 1940s Baltimore.

His family and his home were nothing more than detached black holes to him.

"I remember it like it was yesterday, waiting for my cousin Mitzi to pick me up in her blue Packard convertible," Dick said. "I don't remember much from back then, but I remember that because it was one of the few bright lights in my youth. She would have been 16, and just gotten her driver's license. I must have been 9-10, six years younger than Mitzi, and I remember sitting on the curb, waiting for her to pick me up and how the minutes dragged by like hours."

Mitzi (85 at the time of this writing in 2018) would drive half an hour each way to pick up her younger cousin. Dick speculated that she would have rather been doing any one of a hundred other things, but he always chuckled at the thought of Mitzi and her influence on his young life.

Stepping up on the running board of that Packard, and slipping into the seat next to Mitzi was like a magic carpet ride that took him far, far away from his home. The wind blew in his hair and he could, for one of the rare times in his childhood, look forward instead of back, forgetting his miserable surroundings—the loneliness that he felt at home.

Christened Marguerite Marino (married name, Villasanta) Mitzi was the only child of Uncle Frank Marino, brother to Dick's mother—"the good uncle," as he came to be known.

Uncle Frank had done well with his life. He lived in a great neighborhood and, in addition to being a prominent surgeon, was a major player in the political landscape of Baltimore in those days. His mansion was situated on ten acres outside of Baltimore's Inner City and included beautiful gardens, a bowling alley, ponies, and a swimming pool—paradise to a young, troubled boy.

More than that, the home was filled with memorabilia depicting the history of the Marino family, highlighting its Italian heritage. This was in stark contrast to Dick's home, where no evidence of their Italian heritage could be found.

Dick recalled that "Mitzi was the only daughter of my uncle Frank, who was my greatest mentor, my mother's favorite brother, and a man who supported me through thick and thin—medical school and college, and boarding school before that.

"Most of my 15 cousins were completely dysfunctional—in trouble or alcoholics. Mitzi was a real joy to be around. She was my favorite, no question about it. She was the only one of my extended family I ever felt close to. Even though I probably saw less of her than anyone else, she meant everything to me, and still does today."

Home is where you hang your hat. It's just that all hats weren't created equal. Nevertheless, before his father went into the navy, the Virgilio children didn't suffer from a lack of a roof over their heads. At first they lived with one of Dick's uncles in a row house located in a blue-collar section of Baltimore. These row houses were famous, and Dick spent a lot of time sitting on the front stoop.

"We finally moved into our own home, which was a stand-alone house. It was located on a corner and had a nice yard. My brother and I had our own rooms. We had a telephone with a party line. As

Dick with his mother Rose.

kids, we always picked up and listened in on the conversations. It was great entertainment."

Party lines, as a way of explanation, were a looped local telephone circuit shared by multiple service subscribers. You could get a private line, but it cost more money. Party lines provided a sort of forbidden world at the tip of your phone, where you could overhear gossip between neighboring wives.

"If we weren't listening to the party line, we listened to the radio. We had no TV in those days. I have vague memories of kneeling in the dirt and playing marbles with the guys, but that's about it."

It's difficult to try to imagine life for a young boy back then—a boy in need of parental embrace. All of his immediate needs were met—heat when it was cold, running water, electricity—and the Virgilios weren't rich, but their family never lacked the basic necessities. The only thing lacking, as Dick would reflect upon for the rest of his life, was love, or any resemblance of affection between the four individuals living under that roof.

"I'd describe my family as lower middle class. My parents owned their home, and had a large mortgage on it, as I suppose everyone did at that time. Surprisingly, even though it was my childhood home, I had no real roots in Baltimore, and now I find I've preserved very few memories of that time as there was just no love in my house to nourish such memories."

The distance separating Dick and his older brother seemed only to widen. His father, too, seemed to grow farther and farther from Dick.

"My mother would always side with my father so I wasn't nice to her, which bothered me immensely in my later years," Dick said. "I'm afraid that my mother died never knowing how much I loved and respected her. Living with my father must have been difficult for her, and my brother and I didn't do anything to make it any easier. I will carry that guilt to my grave."

The Virgilio household was strict. There were no traditions that Dick remembered, or could think back on later in life, things that were commonplace with the raising of his own children, things such as decorating the home with Christmas lights, a Thanksgiving turkey, or Christmas dinner. Likewise, he had no memories of family vacations or even a simple outing.

There were no costumes during Halloween and no Easter egg

hunts. In fact, they seldom took dinner together, probably due to the odd hours the senior Virgilio worked as a surgeon.

"I'm sure we had a Christmas tree every year, because my grand-parents would come down from Brooklyn. My mother would always cook Italian sweets and pizzas. I don't remember believing in Santa Claus, or running out to look under the tree Christmas morning, or a first bike or a toy train … or any bike for that matter. It's entirely pos-sible I just suppressed all those remembrances, but I have no memory of them today."

One of the rare pleasant memories of his youth was his mother's cooking.

"… and there was a constant smell of sauce. You could smell it a mile away."

"At home, my mother cooked all the meals. She was your typi-cal old Italian lady who really knew how to cook Italian food. Pasta! On New Year's she cooked a lot of veal dishes, a lot of lasagnas, a lot of raviolis. She would cut the dough and make individual ravioli by hand. My favorite was meat ravioli.

"On New Year's Eve she would always make these cheese piz-zas she called 'cook a la fritte,' My mother was a very, very good cook, having learned from her mother, and she cooked for a large Italian family in her youth. There was no question she reined over her kitchen in our little house.

"I'll never forget. You would walk into the kitchen and there was a constant smell of sauce. You could smell it a mile away. It was always there, even when I was 50 years old and my mother would come out and visit. That's how I knew she was there. I'd come home from work, open the door, and she would have a pot of something boiling on the stove. Instantly my mind would race back years and years to that strange little kitchen of my youth."

* * *

America was a melting pot of immigrants from around the world at that time. While many came to the United States and remained close with others from the old country—choosing to find security in numbers—many others chose to assimilate into American society as rapidly as they could, turning their backs on traditions and languages they had grown up with. Nowhere was this more evident than in Dick's father. He went out of his way to turn his back on his Italian ancestry, even going so far as to change his name from DiVirgilio to Virgilio.

Religion was perhaps the exception, but not for the Virgilios. Although they came from a strict Italian Catholic upbringing, spiritual life in America was different for them.

"My father, and even his parents before him, despite being born in Italy, gave up Catholicism and became Protestant when they came to America, which I always thought was highly unusual. No one would ever talk about why, but, even though my father didn't attend church, he was brought up in the Protestant faith.

"My mother continued to practice Catholicism, and that's where we made our first communion. I don't think we ever received our confirmation. We would go to church on Sundays with my mother, but my father would only attend at Christmas, if then."

A home is usually made up of a series of emotional anchors, things that you count on and look forward to on a daily basis, traditions and furnishings that remind you where you are, smells, comfortable surroundings that tend to have a grounding effect on you. While the Virgilio home was far from a typical American family, it too had things that one could count on daily—things you could set your clock to.

One of the constants Dick came to depend on, as mentioned earlier, was that his mother would always be slaving over the stove when he came home from school. Other, less memorable constants were that his brother would ignore him or pick on him, and that his father would berate him, squashing what little self-esteem or short-lived confidence the boy had endeavored to build.

"Just as I knew my mother was there from the food smells coming from the kitchen, I knew my father was there because of the tension in the air. He was antagonistic and always upset about something.

"As a kid, the only way I could survive was to block out those memories of my father. Essentially, the only things I remember about my life in Baltimore, growing up in those early eight or ten years of my life, were visits to cousin Mitzi's house, and when I belted that little girl who made fun of my stuttering (in first grade), and when my father hit me."

Memories, however, are often like water held back by a dam. The more you talk about the past, the more you remember. You start with a tiny hole in the dike, then the floodwaters begin to rage. Dick was no exception.

"My father came out and hit the guy. He punched him out."

One incident in particular stuck in his mind. "The guy who lived behind us would get mad because we would bounce the ball off the garage door. He came out and hollered at us one day, and that was the only time I ever saw my father lose it.

"My father was a little guy, but he came out and hit the neighbor. He punched him out. The guy was a big guy, too, but down he went. My father had grown up in a rough part of New York and obviously knew how to handle himself in a fight."

Without actually admitting it, Dick may have been just a bit proud of his father that day.

* * *

We go through stages in life. Dick Virgilio, at this time, was restless and always looking to get into trouble. He hung out with a local gang of street punks—kids like him, who had perpetual chips on their shoulders.

He would steal things he neither needed nor wanted, going out of his way to shame his father, because that was the only weapon the young Virgilio seemed to have in his quiver that he felt he could genuinely hurt his father with.

He was a textbook case of conflicted priorities, no self-esteem, and, worse, he was trapped in a house where love, like a flower, died from lack of sunlight and nourishment.

American but thoroughly Italian, smart but berated at every turn, craving acceptance but treated only with repugnance. What options did a small boy have in that world?

"Early in my life, my main objective was to be a failure, so that my father would never be proud of me. I didn't want their pride. To make matters worse, for some reason I wanted my brother to succeed so they would be proud of him, but not of me." It was an era filled with a lot of pain and confusion, influenced by those oft-spoken Italian customs and life on the streets of Baltimore.

"Maybe that's why I don't have many memories of that house. Everyone loved my mother and no one could stand my father.

"He was not easy to like, because he was so full of himself. He was an officer and a doctor, and anybody below him—whether separated by military rank, serving under him as hospital staff, or just the people at his golf club—he felt he was better than. My father wasn't nice to anyone he deemed below his status.

"Yet, he would go to great extremes to impress or suck up to higher-ups, especially if he thought it might get him a little further along in life. It was humiliating to watch, and I was embarrassed to go anywhere with my father."

The year was 1948. As all of this came to a head, no one could have imagined what would happen next.

THREE

New Horizons

As an eleven-year-old, Dick Virgilio hadn't seen much of anything outside of Baltimore. Little did he know then, but when his father came home from work that day in 1948, events were put in motion that would rearrange his destiny and allow him to achieve heights no Virgilio had experienced before.

His father walked in and announced that he would have to abandon his medical practice in Baltimore and fly to the West Coast for deployment overseas.

Dick's father, Frank, had joined the U.S. Navy Reserve and, with the outbreak of hostilities in Korea, he had received orders to report for active duty. He went in kicking and screaming, Dick said, but ended up staying in the Navy for 25 years.

Frank had arranged for housing for his family in Long Beach, California, where Dick and his mother would soon join him. Dick's older brother, Frank Junior, elected to stay with one of his mother's brothers — an uncle in the Baltimore area — using school as his justification.

While the senior Virgilio was transitioning into his new Navy duties, young Dick and his mother were booked on a navy transport ship headed south for the Panama Canal and on to California.

"Seeing the Pacific Ocean for the first time,
and living on the edge of it, wow."

"Going on a ship, through the Panama Canal, was a big deal," Dick recalled. "I was pretty excited. They had movie theaters on the ship, and a swimming pool, so for two weeks at sea I was in heaven. It was an old, World War II troop carrier, but the military used it to transport dependents back and forth from one coast to the other.

"It may have been just an old gray troop transport, but it was like a cruise ship to me. There were lots of other kids on board, too. We took all our meals together and were served by uniformed ship stewards.

"I guess it was cheaper for the navy to just throw us all together on this old troop ship rather than pay all of those families for transportation, mileage, and everything else. They even transported our family car."

How amazing it must have been to see Dick's young face as he gazed upon the Pacific Ocean for the first time—watched the sun set into the water for the first time.

"Seeing the Pacific, and living on the edge of it, wow. It was all very exciting. I swam all the time. We didn't surf because Long Beach was inside the breakwater, but we swam every day, looked at the girls in their bathing suits (I was just at the age where little boys begin to notice such things). But, again, I had no significant relationships with other kids, adults, or mentors. And my father was totally out of the picture."

Dick and his mother got along well.

"I think she was more relieved than I was that my father was gone. We had a great adventure together in Long Beach, even though I'm sure I drove her crazy. She never knew where I was, and I would run off at night doing this or that, and trying to get into trouble. Fortunately, I never got arrested or in real trouble in Long Beach. And for the life of me I don't know why. It was by the grace of God that I didn't. It was just the two of us, and that was great.

"I became a health freak and worked out all the time. My mother bought me some weights, and I created a complete gym, with equipment and everything. I buffed up. I was strong. I don't know why I got into weights. No one ever told me I needed to bulk up, but it gave me something to do, and I liked it.

"Thinking back now, perhaps it was because I never felt very popular. I always considered myself on the periphery of groups that I ran with—both on the streets of Baltimore and on the sand at Long Beach.

"I never felt comfortable in relationships with girls, either. My self-image was not good, and I always felt that girls were not attracted to me. Maybe that's why I wanted to buff up.

"I was impatient. Physical changes came slowly and I just didn't see them. It was like watching a plant grow, or your children. You don't see the daily changes, but when you go away and come back later, growth is evident. My self-esteem would have to wait, it seemed."

In 1949–50, the population of Long Beach was predominantly European-American and 97 percent white. The city was nicknamed "Iowa by the Sea," or "Iowa under Palm Trees," as it had a slower pace than that of neighboring Los Angeles.

During that second half of the 20th century, the city became a major port of entry for Asian and Latin American immigrants headed to Los Angeles. The harbor section of downtown Long Beach was once home to people of Dutch, Greek, Italian, Maltese, Portuguese, and Spanish ancestry; most of them were employed in manufacturing and fish canneries until the 1960s.

"I couldn't have been happier."

"We had rented an apartment right on the beach, at 1000 East Ocean Boulevard, adjacent to a little wrap-around building called the Pacific Club. It was a temporary home. My brother was in Baltimore and my father in Korea. So it was just my mother and I living in this apartment. I couldn't have been happier."

His father was a surgeon onboard the cruiser USS Manchester. Those were the days when naval power was huge. Battleships, which would soon be mothballed, would line up offshore and lob shells at the enemy, a naval tactic dating back to the Napoleonic Wars.

Dick enrolled in Orange Middle School in Long Beach, attending seventh grade.

"Living on the beach was fun. I could walk to school. In fact, I visited there in 2015 to try to find the school. I found the apartment house where we lived, but couldn't find the school. I took woodshop and built a little stool."

That memento of his youth is still part of his home furnishings today.

"Like Baltimore, I didn't have any real close friends in Long Beach. I kept to myself as best as possible and didn't let anyone get close to me—no best friends, no pals. I hung with a group of kids, but, despite the many crazy adventures we had together, I couldn't tell you who any of them were today."

* * *

There was a boardwalk near where the Virgilios lived. Where the marinas are today, there was a huge amusement park called the Pike.

The Pike was built around an enormous wooden rollercoaster, a large plunge, and nearly 200 exhibit booths and rides. Everywhere Dick turned were shooting galleries, pinball machines, merry-go-rounds, spinners, twisters, and carnies hawking their wares—heaven for a young boy.

Meanwhile, young lovers rode the Ferris wheel and fat women stood in front of the distortion mirrors that made them look skinny. Half a century before Disneyland, it was the place to be. The Pike was built in 1902 and remained a presence in Long Beach until 1979.

It was a paradise for families and young children in the daytime, and a hangout for gangs of older kids at night. While still keeping his distance from close relationships, Dick quickly made friends and admirers, even if they weren't the best kids in the neighborhood.

The Pike was also the name of a wooden boardwalk that connected the Pine Street incline to the Long Beach Pier. The "Walk of a Thousand Lights," as it was called, was illuminated with strings of electric lights. This was where Dick and his mother lived.

"That was where everybody hung out—all the guys, all the criminals. We would all hang out either on the boardwalk or at the Pike. We used to call the older Mexican gang members 'Pachucos.'

"In the daytime, I hung out with my school buddies, but, for some reason, I became friends with the older Pachucos. I used to sneak out and go down to the Pike every night and just hang out with the big boys."

The kids he ran with all had tattoos of the cross. One night he got talked into getting one, as a form of gang initiation, but when they started putting it on his ankle, he changed his mind half way through.

"I don't know why I chickened out, but they never finished it."

He lifted his pants leg to show the half-finished tattoo on his left ankle. Today it's just half an inch of the vertical section of the cross, dark blue, and another incomplete memory of his youth.

"They really were a bunch of bad kids, far more so than the guys I ran around with in Baltimore. They robbed stores, and it seemed their plans just kept getting more and more serious in a criminal direction. I think I got scared of the whole scene. I didn't want to be a follower and get into real trouble, but it could've easily happened.

"I've been fortunate throughout my life to have had lots of mentors—good people who watched out for me. I had no one like that in Long Beach. I was lucky to get away from that group. The half tattoo certainly reminds me of that today."

It also demonstrated that, even at such an early age, Dick Virgilio, the stubborn Italian kid from Baltimore, wasn't about to be pushed into anything, unless he wanted it.

Except for a side trip to San Diego with his mother to tend to Dick's broken arm, Long Beach was his permanent residence. "I don't remember how I broke my arm, but my mother and I drove to San Diego to see a specialist and what I do remember about that trip is taking the old car-carrying ferryboat to Coronado. That must have been about 1950."

* * *

His father's deployment seemed to end far too soon for the younger Virgilio. When the USS Manchester hove into the Port of Long Beach in June of 1950, he and his mother were there to greet it. As they drove down the Navy wharf, Dick could feel the tension growing in his gut—the stress flooding back into his life. He was definitely not happy to see his father. Naturally, there were no hugs, and, most certainly, there were no, "I love you and missed you" sentiments shared.

Wasting no time, the senior Virgilio packed up the family car and left California for a drive across country to his new duty station— Portsmouth Naval Hospital in Virginia. It was just the three of them, with Dick pouting in the backseat the entire drive—a 40-hour drive of nearly 3,000 miles.

Whether consciously or subconsciously, Dick studied the road signs along the way in what was probably his only form of entertainment. This mental mapping of his route was instinctive, and that awareness of his surroundings soon came into play.

There was no air conditioning back then, all the windows were rolled down, and day by day that car took him farther from where he wanted to be—and closer to his new personal hell.

"Most kids would be thrilled to see their father after such a separation, but not me. In my mind, all I could think about was how I was going to get away from him. And for me to go from Long Beach and the Pacific Ocean to hot and muggy Portsmouth and all those mosquitoes was just something I couldn't imagine. I hated Portsmouth. I hated my father."

It's funny, how the mind of a young boy works at that age.

"I was just thirteen, and there were no child labor laws, so, as we drove into Portsmouth, I saw a sign in a store window that said 'Help

Wanted.' I made my mother stop the car, and I went in to talk to the owner. I got a job at thirteen in a grocery store. Can you imagine that today?

"I didn't work in Long Beach, but in Virginia I could make forty cents an hour. I'll never forget that. I stocked shelves, cleaned floors, and I suppose I always worked from that time forward. I was never very skilled at anything, but I always found jobs. It didn't matter what I did or what I got paid, as long as I was far away from my father."

FOUR

Adventure Awaits

Television, although primarily a pastime of the upper middle class, rapidly caught on in the post-World War II period. "I Love Lucy" premiered on CBS in 1948, and the black and white TV established its place as the most important single form of entertainment during the ensuing decade.

In 1950, the average American family income was $3,700 a year. The average cost of a new house was $9,000, and the price of gas was 12 cents a gallon. Nuclear bomb tests were taking place in Nevada and direct-dial, coast-to-coast telephone service was available.

None of that mattered to Dick Virgilio. By early August in the summer of 1950, the Virgilios were back on the east coast. Long Beach was but a distant memory. Portsmouth was 238 miles south of Baltimore, but it was the same hell to him.

"We got to Portsmouth that June, and I got a job right away. I worked hard. I didn't know anybody because we hadn't lived there before, and school hadn't started yet, so I poured myself into my job. I worked as a stock boy and janitor in a local grocery store. My salary was 40 cents an hour and I worked all the hours I could get."

Working full-time put some money in Dick's pocket and kept him from having to deal with his father, or so he hoped. Yet, it was a given that, when the Virgilio men were all under one roof, things heated up.

The berating, the punishment, and the constant criticism continued. Having just turned 13, Dick had had enough—and he believed he was old enough to do something about it.

"I can't say there was any one thing that caused me to run away. It was an accumulation of a lot of stuff—unhappiness and a lot of me wanting to do things, and he not wanting to let me do them. Today, kids run away for a lot of reasons—maybe because they're being abused. Maybe their parents are on drugs. I just hated my father, hated my home, and hated everything he represented."

The world was shrinking. The Virgilio household was shrinking too, especially for one 13-year-old boy.

"All I had was three dollars and seventy-five cents and a couple of T-shirts."

"At the end of that summer, my father and I had this falling out. I ran away. I was scared to death. My brother was living with us for a time, and I don't recall whether he was going to stay with us or go back to Baltimore with my uncle.

"I still looked up to my older brother at that time, so I went to him and told him I was going to run away. He said, 'What are you telling me for?' I was hoping he would talk me out of it, but he didn't. He just said, 'Have a good trip.' I never felt more alone or less loved in my life, but I was determined to start my journey and not look back.

"My running away from home was the result of a big confrontation with my father that just made me snap. I had gone a full year without seeing him, and all of a sudden I had to live with him again, under the same roof. I had, I suppose, grown some myself in his absence, both physically and mentally. I had learned that my mother and I could do just fine without him. We didn't need him."

John Wayne once said, "Courage is being scared to death but saddling up anyway." Well, young Dick Virgilio was about to find out what courage was all about.

"So, I just climbed out the window in the middle of the night with a little canvas bag that contained a pair of football shoes I had bought with my work money. They were the old cleats we all used to wear back then, and they must have been particularly important to me because I had worked so hard to buy them. I remember I was about to start high school and wanted to play football.

"I put those cleats in the bag and started off. All I had was three dollars and seventy-five cents and a couple of T-shirts. My brother wouldn't give me any money, and he didn't give a shit whether I stayed or went.

"So I took off. I slipped out the window and walked for what seemed like forever, through a terrible part of town in an all-black neighborhood. Eventually, I got to the highway. I can still remember how dark it was, and how really, really scared I was.

"I got to the highway, stuck my thumb out, and began hitchhiking. I didn't know how far I'd get, but I did sort of know the way we had come when driving cross-country. I was old enough to know a little— I had a map, and I knew the main highways. I also knew that the sun set in the west, and that was about it.

"Once I reached the highway, it was just one traumatic adventure after another— being stranded in the mountains of Tennessee, people throwing me out of their car, rides dropping me off suddenly and leaving me in the middle of the night."

Hitchhiking, which originated in America, became popular with the advent of the automobile, and really hit its stride during the Great Depression. By the 1950s, Dick had, no doubt, heard plenty of hitch-hiking nightmares—gruesome stories about kidnapping, torture, decapitation, and even ritual sacrifice.

"My mind was filled with scenarios in which physical harm would come to me."

Still, young Dick clomped on into the dark of night. He may not have known what lay ahead, but he knew what lay behind, and he was finished with that.

* * *

The art of hitchhiking is simple. You position yourself on a busy thoroughfare, face the oncoming traffic, and put your right thumb in the air, pointing the direction you are headed.

After the first dozen cars pass you by, little tricks begin to seep into your routine. Perhaps you try to look tougher; perhaps you want the innocent look, so as to appeal to families driving by.

Whatever you do, you never want to show fear; always hitch-hike with confidence. Eye contact is important, because if you do get picked up by a weirdo, that's where the first clue will be—in the eyes.

Maybe you inject a little motion in your wrist or elbow to enhance your dire circumstance. Claudette Colbert, in the hit 1934 film, "It Happened One Night," hoists her skirt, revealing a sexy leg. No thumb necessary for her.

Whatever the technique, there is always that moment when someone slows down to pick you up, you run to the passenger side, and then deal with your fears before you open the door and place yourself at the mercy of this complete stranger.

As you lean in the window, you and the driver assess the situation simultaneously. Usually the driver says, "Where ya headed?" At that point you're just so damned relieved to be off your feet and moving in a car that your fears disappear and you focus once more on your destination. In Dick's case, his destination was Long Beach, California.

"I was really scared."

"I wound up in Tennessee, at the other end of Nashville. A young couple picked me up, and they took me fifty, sixty miles out of town, then stopped the car and said, 'This is as far as we're going. Get out.' So I got out. It was pitch black dark. I was in the middle of nowhere. And I could hear the dogs barking and wolves baying in the hills around me. I was really scared.

"Eventually, I saw these truck lights coming down the road, going the other way. I knew there was a city behind me, so I flagged him down. The guy took me back to where I had just left. I slept on a park bench that night and hung out until morning, when I started off again."

That cold night on a hard and lonely park bench, jumping at every noise, Dick had plenty to think about. Okay, he had run away. Technically, he had won. He walked out of his father's life and saw a little of the world on his own. It would have been easy for anyone else to turn around at that point and go back. Not Dick Virgilio. Even though he was but a few hundred miles from home, he was past the point of no return.

"In the morning I decided there was no way I was going back home, that's for sure. The next thing I really remember about that adventure was in Texas. I had developed this cock-and-bull story about what I was doing out there. Nobody believed me, I'm sure, but I had this story, and it changed every day.

"One day I'd say that my parents had sent me to California for school. The next day I'd say that I was visiting family there. Whatever I would say, I stressed that my parents had 'authorized' the trip, and that my parents thought it would be a 'great adventure' for me. Runaways weren't a big deal in the 1950s, and hitchhiking was an accepted mode of transportation.

"About that time, this preacher picked me up. He said he thought I looked hungry. Well, I was hungry. I was hungry all the time, because I didn't want to spend what little money I had.

"I left with three dollars and seventy-five cents, and I think I arrived in California with two dollars of that. People would buy me meals and sometimes give me a little money along the way. This preacher took me to his house and said he was gonna have his wife make me a meal. Then I heard him on the phone calling the police, saying he had a runaway there. Before he finished his call, I was out the door and gone. I never did get dinner.

"But we had driven off the highway to get to his house, and I didn't know where I was. So I had to somehow find my way back to the highway. I finally did.

"The next real thing I remember is having a trucker pick me up in New Mexico and take me all the way to Los Angeles. He had a big bed in back of his cab and let me sleep up there. He bought me all my meals and dropped me right on the waterfront, not far from where I had lived before. I felt comfortable at that point of the journey, because I had just spent a year in Los Angeles and Long Beach.

"So, three thousand miles later, and even more because of all the detours and side trips, I finally got to Long Beach. I knew exactly who to find when I hitchhiked in. There were all these kids I had hung around with on my first trip to the West Coast, and I knew where to find them.

"To my surprise, they were really excited to see me and began feeding me and bringing me clothes and sleeping bags. These were my former school buddies, not the gang of older kids at the Pike. These kids seemed to really have respect for me, right or wrong. They should've labeled me a dumbass and called the police, but they didn't.

"I would sleep on park benches or on the beach, or anywhere prying eyes couldn't see me. I never went to their houses and I never slept in a shelter. It was the end of summer, September, and the weather was good. The worst weather in Long Beach is rain every once in awhile.

"I'm sorry to say I don't remember any of the names of those kids who did so much to keep me fed and sheltered. I don't know why, but I sort of became a hero to those Long Beach kids. They had never met anyone, kid or adult, who had hitchhiked across country.

"In those days, in Long Beach, there was an open kitchen where all the homeless guys would go to get a free meal. I could go there once or twice a week, no questions asked. I was the youngest fellow there. I ate with the homeless a couple of days a week. My priorities were simple at that point—food and shelter.

"My meals were supplemented by what the kids brought me.

Eventually, one of their mothers noticed food and other stuff disappearing from the house and followed her kid, who inadvertently led her right to me. I was busted.

"The phone calls started, and the next thing I knew I was on an airplane headed back to Baltimore. My friend's mother called my mother, and the mystery of what happened to Dick Virgilio was solved. My three-month vacation was over.

"I'm sure my mother was relieved to hear I was okay, but we never talked about it, not ever. Knowing how close she was to her brother Frank, it's no surprise now, looking back, why he got involved. I don't suppose my own father cared a bit, one way or another."

* * *

In hindsight, Dr. Frank Marino obviously was involved in the search for his nephew, and had begun to create a complicated and expensive option for his wayward nephew. Once Dick had been located, Uncle Frank arranged to get him an airplane ticket home.

"I flew on one of those old prop planes, a Constellation. They had huge wings and four prop engines. Back then it was the biggest plane they flew from coast to coast.

"We stopped in Chicago, and I was still trying to figure out a way to break out and get away. What I didn't realize at the time was that they had warned the stewardess to keep a close eye on me. I tried to talk her into letting me get off the plane, so I could go to the bathroom. My plan was to disappear while in the terminal, but they made me stay on the plane to do my business, which foiled my only opportunity to escape and work my way back to Long Beach.

"We landed in Washington. This entire time I'm still thinking, how can I get away and get back to Long Beach? Little did I know what they had in store for me at that point."

Dick's mother Rose (left), uncle Frank, and cousin Mitzi — three people who had a profound influence on Dick's life.

FIVE

Military School

Dick's mother, Rose Virgilio, was the only girl of seven children born to Rosario and Concetta Marino. She was born in this country. One of her six brothers, Frank Marino, was born in Italy but had become quite successful in America. He and Rose had remained close since early childhood. More than once Rose reached out to him for help with her own children.

"My mother was the light of my many uncles' lives," Dick fondly recalled years later. "She was the only girl in a family of six boys, and she was the youngest. Uncle Frank was not fond of my father, to put it politely, but he would do anything for my mother."

Indeed, Frank Marino worshipped his sister and, being the most successful of the Marino brothers, he stood by her side through thick and thin. He was the great watchdog, the safety net, and the proverbial big brother—always looking over her, and, in some cases, looking over her youngest son, Dick.

In 1951, near the end of what turned out to be a miserably long and hot summer, young Dick Virgilio was found in California—a runaway who two months earlier had disappeared without a trace.

While there is no known record or Missing Child Report for Dick Virgilio, it is assumed that his mother and uncle carried the brunt of the worry. Uncle Frank arranged for his nephew to be flown, under the strict supervision of the flight crew, from Long Beach to Washington, D.C.

At that point, Dick's Uncle Frank took the child's destiny into his own hands, forever realigning Dick's stars.

"When the airplane landed in Washington, Uncle Frank and my mother were there to pick me up. I'm sure my mother was happy to see me, but there was no homecoming, no outward show of affection. If there were tears, they were well disguised. There was no rushing towards one another, no embracing.

"It didn't surprise me that my father wasn't there to greet me. He had remained in Portsmouth, where I ran from. My mother and Uncle Frank were smart enough to realize bringing him would have been a big mistake. Years later I often wondered how aggressive my father had been in looking for me. I never asked. No one ever told me."

"I never went home after that."

Dick's instructions from Uncle Frank were simple: "Get in the car!"

"I had no idea where we were going," Dick said, "but when I got off the plane, I told Uncle Frank I didn't want to go back home. He looked at me and said, 'You're not going back home.' Indeed, I never went home after that.

"We started driving. No one talked. About an hour later, and in the dark, we drove up a hill on a property filled with gray buildings.

"When we stopped, a man in a military uniform opened the door and said, 'Follow me.' My mother kissed me, and my uncle didn't say a word. Only then did I realize that I was going to be there for a while, that I was going to become a student in a military school. Where the hell this school was, or how I would survive this, I had no idea."

His destination, his new home for the foreseeable future, was a strict, military-themed McDonogh School. For Dick Virgilio it was "three strikes," and at that stage in his young life he had no alternatives, no options.

* * *

McDonogh School was created through the estate of John McDonogh, a Baltimore-born merchant and philanthropist who, toward the end of the 19th century, bequeathed half of his estate to the City of Baltimore for the purpose of educating needy children.

In 1872, John McDonogh paid $85,000 to purchase 838 acres as a home for the school. The McDonogh School of today essentially occupies the same land that was originally set aside.

The school was founded in 1873 when 21 poor boys from Baltimore City arrived on campus. Most of those original 21 students were either orphans or missing a parent; a number of them were sons of Civil War veterans. They followed a semi-military system designed to provide structure and leadership opportunities, and to ensure order. That policy continued for many years.

The semi-military program was dropped in 1971 and the school now allows female students and operates as a non-denominational, co-educational college preparatory day school offering five-day boarding options for students.

As it was in the beginning, the school continues to stress moral character, a sense of responsibility, and a capacity for leadership while preparing the students academically for college and beyond.

In the beginning, McDonogh didn't allow just any children to attend (as Baltimore already had a thorough public school system). This school was intended to be for the education of underprivileged students, boys only, and children of "good character."

Once entrenched in the daily regimen of McDonogh, Dick came to realize that most of the children attending the school were actually from affluent homes, and that scholarships were available for the underprivileged.

While Dick met the first two of those requirements — being a boy and considered underprivileged — he was severely lacking in good character. That's where his Uncle Frank stepped in, providing necessary personal references and whatever financial leverage was needed to get his nephew accepted. Surely there were those in the McDonogh hierarchy who had serious doubts about Dick Virgilio.

When Uncle Frank and Dick drove up to the campus, Dick was overwhelmed. He had no idea what was going to happen next, but, even as the car pulled up to this fortress of a military school—what looked to be a gated prison—Dick was already planning how he would escape.

Frank Marino was a very influential man, and he was used to buying his way anywhere he wanted to go. His influence spread throughout the state of Maryland. He owned a substantial amount of commercial property in the Baltimore area, in addition to beautiful homes both there and on the beach in Ocean City, Maryland.

As a doctor during the Depression, he treated everyone. At times people couldn't pay in cash, so he ended up with real estate. He did very well, and he was extremely generous in giving back to his community. And he wielded that influence to help an errant nephew.

Suddenly, Dick found himself in an environment with uniformed instructors and students who would be making most of his decisions for him. For how long, he had no idea. But it was "home"—that much was for certain.

"It was a very prominent school, McDonogh School. At that time, it was all male, military uniforms, very disciplined, and everywhere you went on campus, you marched in cadence.

"Now, all these years later, I realize that my mother could have conversations with her brother she couldn't have with her own husband. In fact, my Uncle Frank was the only person she could turn to. In this instance, despite what I might have thought at the time, Uncle Frank's decision proved to be a good one."

* * *

"I had no suitcase or travel bag," Dick recalled. "Just the clothes I had on—the same clothes I ran away in. They stripped me down and pointed me towards this big room where they had pants and shirts, all military, and said 'try this on, try that on. Try these shoes.' When you went to McDonogh, boarders lived each day in uniform. You didn't need much else.

"Most kids would have been stiff with fear.

Baltimore, Friday, **T**

PAGE 28

Dick Katz, Nicki

DICK VIRGILIO   SANDY DUGAN
Virgilio, Cadet unlimited matman, and 138-pound Dugan, of Gilman, in tonight's match

Wrestling, football and lacrosse were Dick's sports. In 2010 he was inducted in the McDonogh Sports Hall Of Fame.

PAGE 52

Baltimore, Thursday, **THE EVENING SUN**

McDonogh Heft, Speed Gai

It's All In The Viewpoint

Triple A Ball Loops Need Consolidation

By PAUL MENTON

[Sports Editor, The Evening Sun]

Frank Lane and Bill Veeck get the headlines with continued talk of major league baseball in California, but the sport has a bigger, more immediate problem.

That's consolidation and strengthening of top minor loops, the American Association and International League.

At the moment both are down to seven clubs, both have cities no longer capable of successfully supporting Triple A ball with its rising costs and the encroachment of major league interest in their communities.

If baseball men are really interested in the future of their game, every effort should be made to effect a consolidation of the Association and International League into one strong Triple A circuit before next spring.

Unless it comes, there will be further weakening of the game's minor league structure by replacing Kansas City and Ottawa with cities unsound economically. Thus, franchises which rightfully belong in AA or A will be ruined with the financial burdens of AAA clubs, eventually lost to baseball.

No one seriously believes Havana can long survive the financial strain of competing in the International League with its excessive travel costs. Addition of Miami can be only a temporary stopgap.

Difference A Year Can Make

When the American football coaches sit down to select their

DICK VIRGILIO

McDonogh blocking back sharpens his blocks for duel with Gilman

A little press for Dick during football season.

Dick was just plain mad."

"Some kids didn't live on campus, but most did. Some lived at home and commuted. They had a store on campus where you could get toothpaste and that kind of stuff, but it was bare necessities and that's it."

It was mid-session and classes had already started. All of a sudden this tough looking little Italian kid arrives with no uniform, dirty, scruffy, and the look of a caged animal that had just lost his first taste of freedom.

"I was fighting mad. I couldn't figure out why they were going to put me into this military school. But my mind started working right away, thinking, how am I gonna break out of this place?"

By the time they dropped him off, word was already traveling throughout the students and teachers about this runaway kid from California.

"It took a lot of money to stay there and, except for the students on scholarship, these were all upper-class kids. It was more like a high-end Baltimore boarding school.

"I guess my reputation preceded me. While a lot of that conversation went on behind the scenes, years later I found out my fellow students knew about me.

"There were about 65 kids in my class. At a recent reunion of about 18 of us, some of them told me they were afraid of me in those early days. One fellow said there was a moment he was scared to death. Apparently we were marching and he was behind me. He coughed and a little spittle landed on my back. I never knew, but he said he was sure I was going to turn around and pummel him with my rifle butt.

"Others told me how they would sit and wait patiently for me to come back from my little campus outings and bring them things. Today we all laugh and celebrate having survived life this long—having survived McDonogh.

"These days McDonogh School is a co-ed school and one of the most gorgeous places you've ever seen—rolling hills, horses. It's located just ten minutes from downtown Baltimore. But in 1950, it was more like a state penitentiary on the outside, with extremely regimented living on the inside. You lived in an open dormitory with maybe 25 other kids. Bunks next to one another like a barracks.

"I didn't know a soul. I was by myself. And I was so lonely. I had nobody. At least when I ran away to Long Beach, I knew some of the boys there. Here I had nobody.

"It was like starting my life all over. I didn't have any family to talk to. My father wouldn't talk to me. My mother lived with him in Portsmouth, Virginia, which was a couple of hundred miles away. I hadn't seen my brother since I ran away, and wouldn't see him for the next five years.

"It was traumatic. I just said, 'Self, you've just got to get your shit together, stop feeling sorry for yourself, and find out what's going on in this place.'

"Number one, I knew I had to get to know somebody. But school had already started. It wasn't like the first day of school, when you meet your teacher and make friends.

"I stuck out like a sore thumb amidst a sea of neatly pressed uniforms. These other kids had already been in their classes for several months. And then there was me, in my stiff, new military clothes, smelling as though they had come straight from the factory, straight from the hanger."

A typical McDonogh day meant getting up at six in the morning to a bugle call. The cadets formed up and took care of all their designated chores, whether it be cleaning out the heads, taking out the garbage, or making beds. Then they marched to breakfast. After they ate, they went to class and were in school all day. Then they had dinner and went to bed. The next day the bugle call launched that schedule all over again, day after day, week after week, month and year after year.

"Being thrust into military school was very traumatic for me," Dick said. "The classes were a lot tougher than what I was used to in public school. It took me several months, but I finally got a feel for the rhythm of the school.

"It was a nice facility. I applied myself early on at my studies. In those days they really didn't have a medical diagnosis for what I had, but I was quick to learn that I had trouble reading. Years later I was diagnosed as being dyslectic.

"I transposed words and letters. I literally couldn't write, couldn't creatively write. But I could memorize, so I faked my way through school. I faked my way through military school and eventually faked my way through medical school.

"I was always good at math. Dyslexia didn't hurt me with numbers. But I was terrible at English, writing, or anything where I had to create or write an essay. It was a nightmare for me. I was a good public speaker. But as far as writing anything, forget it. It just didn't happen.

"In the early 1950s, dyslexia wasn't a common thing. Now, when my son Joe began to demonstrate the same symptoms I had experienced, we knew right away what the problem was, and we got him into a special class. He worked through it, but only because we were on top of it and knew exactly what the problem was.

"Over the years I've written letters to my kids, to my wife Bea, expressing my love and admiration for them. But for every one-page letter written, I probably threw 15 pages in the trash.

"Eventually, I came to realize McDonogh had very good athletic programs. I continued to work out, as I had in Long Beach. I was a freshman the year after I got to McDonogh and started wrestling, and playing football and lacrosse. As an athlete you can't help but gain a little stature and self-esteem. I finally began to see how I could modify the school system to fit in with things I wanted to do.

"For starters, no one was going to lock me up—keep me from going off campus—so I found a way through the woods to get down to this little country store and ended up bringing some stuff back. The other kids wouldn't risk leaving the campus, so I would collect their money and go down and bring shit back for them—food items, mostly. Submarine sandwiches were really popular."

An entrepreneur of the greatest magnitude, Dick would take money from the guys, buy the goods, and then keep some for himself.

"I didn't have a license at that point, but the school let me drive the trash truck. Everyone had a job to do in the morning. That was mine. I had two guys working for me, and we would drive this big old trash truck around the campus, picking up all the trashcans, and then we would drive to the dump.

"The dump was still on campus, which is probably why they allowed me to drive without a license, but was a couple miles down the road. We dumped the trash, and then had a cigarette. We kept our cigarettes hidden there.

"When I turned sixteen, they let me get my driver's license and they had me driving off campus in the carryalls—the large school vans.

* * *

Dick had never experienced anything like McDonogh School. It's probably safe to assume that the McDonogh School had never experienced anyone like Dick Virgilio, before or since.

"On Saturday nights the boarders who lived on campus would be allowed a movie. To get the movie someone had to pick up the film reels at the Pikes Theatre in Pikesville, about ten miles off campus. They were huge thirty-five-millimeter reels—usually three reels to a movie. So I'd load the containers of film into the van and, on the way back, I'd stop at the stores and pile on sodas, candy, and things like that. Then I'd sell product to the kids for a profit. That's how I made money."

There really wasn't any need for Dick to buy anything at the school. His Uncle Frank had taken care of the tuition, books, and uniforms, but early on Dick developed a way to satisfy two very important needs—one was to get freedom, and the other was to make money.

He became the senior driver on campus, usually driving the large '52 Chevy panel van, filled with rows of seats. When kids had doctor appointments, they would call Dick to drive them. The four-wheel-drive van had a standard three-speed manual transmission (three in the tree), manually initiated drive in the front hubs, and a compound low—a young man's dream, and one heck of a first vehicle to learn to drive in. It was virtually indestructible.

Dick drove the movie run. Movies were usually first-run films such as "From Here to Eternity," "House of Wax," "On the Waterfront," and "Godzilla." One can only imagine a room filled with cadets, eyes fixed on the makeshift movie screen and screaming in unison as

Godzilla climbed out of the ocean. Dick also had the enviable job of being the projectionist.

"I always felt the more I could do, the more I could get away with. So I learned how to run this crazy projector. In those days one reel would end and everyone had to wait while you put the second reel on. And then it would flick and skip until the film caught hold. Meanwhile, everyone would be screaming at me and yelling for the movie.

"After the movie, I had to take the film back to the theater. So we would show the movie right after dinner, say at seven p.m. Then, about nine p.m., I would be driving ten miles down the road to take the movie back. But I didn't mind. That gave me another chance to provision for the guys.

"There was this one little store on the night run that would sell beer to me. I was shocked I was able to get away with that. I was all of sixteen years old, but I would buy cases of beer and take it back to sell to the guys.

"The drinking age in Washington, DC, was 18, and the drinking age across the state line in Maryland was 21. So it was not easy to buy booze. But, you're out there in the country, and these little country stores could care less. There were no video cams watching, or people checking your ID.

"McDonogh had a bed check every night. The guys always wanted to go with me to return the films, but we would have to figure a way to get them checked into their bed before they could sneak out with me. It was a crazy time."

Eventually Dick and his cronies learned to siphon gas out of vehicles on campus and put it in a friend's car.

He laughed at the recollection. "No matter how careful you were, you got a mouthful of gas."

SIX

A Friend Indeed

Students who boarded at McDonogh School generally lived in or around the Baltimore/Washington area. They went home for the weekends, leaving just a small core of guys—students who didn't have a home to go to—to occupy the enormous campus.

Boys like Dick never went home. In fact, he believes he may hold the record for length of time living on campus.

Boarding students could apply for weekend passes to go to another student's home. At one point, Bob Royer invited Dick to his farm—but what out West would be called a "cattle ranch." That led to Dick living with the Royers during the summer, where he worked on their farm, earning money in the process.

Dick and Bob became best friends. Later, Bob served as Dick's best man when he met and married Bea, years later. The two men have remained close to this day.

"I began to visit Bob Royer in my sophomore year, about 1953-54. To this day I don't know what inspired Bob to invite me home with him. I know at school we would talk, and one day he just said, 'Why don't you come out to the house for the weekend?' I figured, why not—anything to get off the campus. And the only way you could get out is if you had a place to go and an adult to sign for you."

"I was so jealous of this family."

Bob Royer was not in the same year/class as Dick, but at McDonogh there was no caste system amongst the students. They were all in it together.

"I started going to their farm when I was sixteen or seventeen and never stopped. Bob was a year behind me, but I spent every summer and holiday there, and that was where I learned about what a real family was. The farm was only about a twenty-five-minute drive from campus, but the two were worlds apart.

"I was so jealous of this family in the beginning, and then I wasn't jealous any longer because I was a part of it. It took me about a year of going out to the farm on weekends and holidays before I understood how different it was. I woke up one morning and realized they had been treating me like one of their own sons.

"They had two boys, and then they had me. When I screwed up, however, they let me know I was wrong. And yet, it wasn't the same feeling of screwing up at my own house. At my house it never went well with my father. If I did something wrong or thoughtless at the Royers' house, it quickly became a learning experience on what not to do.

"In my own house, I would purposely be bad just to get my father upset; if I did it in their house I really felt awful about it. I cared a great deal for the Royers."

The Royer farm was 640 acres. What a contrast it was to the regimentation of the school. And here, like school, there were regular chores to be done.

Chores included helping feed the cattle, bringing in hay bales, moving the cattle around, cleaning the barn and the grounds. There was something to be done every day of the week.

And yet, somehow these chores seemed more worthwhile, even meaningful. They seemed to feed a latent hunger in Dick to do well and impress his elders. He actually cared what the Royers thought about him.

"I had never been on a farm before. I wasn't sure how I was going to like it, and I learned to love it. I have so many fond memories of family life there, whereas I didn't have any before. It was a very important chapter in my life. It was a real eye-opener for me."

* * *

Dick's visiting the farm was an eye-opener for the Royers as well, as Bob Royer recollected many years later.

"My first memory of Dick was of this guy who showed up at McDonogh School wearing Levis, no belt loops, white T-shirt rolled up over these muscular arms. He looked like a deer in the headlights," said Bob.

"McDonogh was a great school. It turned Dick's life around and did the same thing for me. It set us on wonderful career paths and helped us build great foundations for our lives to come. Clearly Dick was standing at the crossroads, with his direction meter heading him in the wrong direction. Yes, McDonogh really turned him around.

"The guy who ran the school back then was Louis 'Doc' Lamborn. He was the headmaster and literally the maker of young men. He always had a couple of people to whom he paid a lot of attention. Dick and I were fortunate to be two of Doc's special kids.

"At that time, McDonogh was a military school, from a discipline standpoint. It was not associated with the military or the government, but they ran it with a strict military-inspired disciplinary system.

"Everybody at McDonogh wore the same uniform, made by the same company, so we all looked alike. It didn't matter whether or not you could afford a Vicuña cashmere sport coat or denim sport jacket; we all wore the same clothes.

"Dick and I were on several of the same sports teams—football, lacrosse, wrestling. I think the catalyst that drew us close together, however, was when we were dating girls who went to the same college.

They both attended St. Mary's College, which was just outside of Baltimore.

"Those two girls became very good friends. One of them lived just four farms away from where I lived. So that probably is what drew us close together at first. And that's probably what brought Dick to our home early on.

"Our farm was called Bushy Park Farm. We raised *Polled Herefords* as a registered cattle business, designed to improve the commercial cattle industry by creating better yields and a better quality of beef.

"We had someone to work the farm, and another worker to tend the cattle. Depending on the time of year and the work required, there were a few more. I worked on the farm all my life, as did my brothers. When Dick visited, he worked, too. While on the farm, we would get up early and help with the chores.

"We had three meals a day and always ate together. A typical breakfast was a whole lot of eggs, bacon, sausage, toast, and scrapple (pan rabbit—a mush of pork scraps and trimmings combined with cornmeal, wheat flour, and spices). For lunch we ate soup and sandwiches, mostly.

"At dinner we primarily ate beef in one fashion or another. At the dinner table there could be as few as four of us or as many as eight. Our home was home for the workers as well. Every holiday their families would come to our place and spend Christmas, Thanksgiving, and Easter. This was all new to Dick, but he fit right in, and my parents loved him dearly.

"My dad had a very relaxed personality, but was always extremely successful, whether it was the cattle business, insurance, transportation, or real estate. He never touched anything that he either didn't own or run at the very top of the organization at some point.

"When you find someone like that, who is easy to talk to, easy to be in a relationship with, somewhat humble, and yet so obviously successful, it's no wonder that Dick was drawn to him. Dick was extremely hungry for that sort of a fatherly relationship. My father ended up walking Dick's future wife, Bea, down the aisle. They were that close. And Dick introduced me to my wife, Jo. We were, and are, that close."

* * *

About that time, at age 17 and a senior at McDonogh, Dick joined the U.S. Navy Reserve. In the Reserve, he started out at the bottom, as a seaman first class. He went to submarine school and became part of a submarine reserve unit while in Baltimore. Dick said his motivation

Best Athlete
DICK VIRGILIO
Voted best athlete by his classmates.

for joining the Reserve was just to give him another opportunity to leave the campus once a month.

He attended meetings and served on submarines for two months during the summer. Even when attending college, he served two months a year on a submarine. He stayed with that program, and that helped him a great deal when he retired from the navy.

"I always wanted to be a doctor."

For all intents and purposes, it seemed as if Dick Virgilio was setting a positive course for his future by juggling graduation from McDonogh, preparing to enter college, and still keeping his Naval Reserve status active. Granted, he continued to make his off-campus runs, supplying food and drink to the other students and supplementing his meager income.

"Getting into the navy at the age of seventeen was the best thing I ever did. All that time helped me through pay purposes, and it was another life experience that helped me understand certain things; it helped me grow to be a little more independent; it helped me realize you have to work with other people.

"It was a life-changing experience. It also allowed me to gain more time towards my retirement, which proved to be financially very beneficial later in my life.

"The funny thing is that I always wanted to be a doctor. My relationship with my father was actually holding me back as I struggled between what I wanted, and what I thought he might have wanted."

Once Dick got used to the routine at McDonogh, and his self-esteem began to improve, he started to open his eyes and see the bigger picture. As a bit of an epiphany for someone so young, Dick discovered the world wasn't such a bad place after all. In fact, he was delighted to find that some of his teachers and coaches on campus actually liked him, trusted him, and most of all encouraged him.

"The McDonogh teachers were like family to me. They lived on campus. Most were younger folks with small kids of their own and lived in campus apartments.

"I latched on to relationships with them, just like I latched on to Bob Royer and his family, because I never felt like I had my own family. It was exciting for me to have them invite me into their homes and treat me like one of their family, knowing that basically I was just some wayward kid."

One such relationship was with his football coach, Dick Working, and his wife and three kids. Dick Working was the housefather in the senior dormitory. The Workings frequently invited Dick for dinner on weekends.

"There were three or four people like that, like Dick Working, who really began to change my whole attitude towards life. None of

Dick, captain of the football team.

them could break my anger and hatred for my father, nor could they completely change my efforts to fail because of him, but they gave me such great security and comfort.

"I began to realize that some people do have nice families. They worry about their families. They're close to each other. They aren't

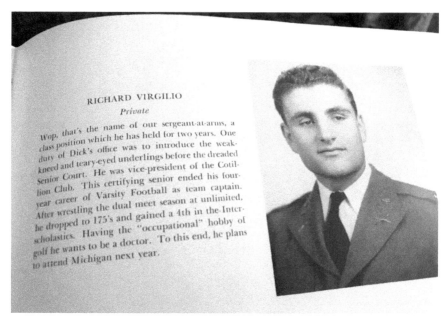

RICHARD VIRGILIO
Private

Wop, that's the name of our sergeant-at-arms, a class position which he has held for two years. One duty of Dick's office was to introduce the weak-kneed and teary-eyed underlings before the dreaded Senior Court. He was vice-president of the Cotillion Club. This certifying senior ended his four-year career of Varsity Football as team captain. After wrestling the dual meet season at unlimited, he dropped to 175's and gained a 4th in the Inter-scholastics. Having the "occupational" hobby of golf he wants to be a doctor. To this end, he plans to attend Michigan next year.

McDonogh School yearbook 1956.

afraid to express their love for each other. They celebrate things and have traditions—things that I had never experienced growing up.

"I grew to be very close to them, as well as their young children. As I got older, sixteen, seventeen, eighteen, and still living on campus, I began to babysit for them, so they could go out to dinner or a movie. They were literally my extended families.

"All in all there must have been three couples that lived on campus, and they were all coaches of mine. Another was a teacher who didn't coach but became quite influential. They made my life bearable. Between time spent with them, and with the Royers, and the various jobs I had taken on, and my sports involvement, I kept too busy to be miserable."

"Dick never once backed down against the rushing strength of Jim Brown."

Bob Royer recalled, "Dick never seemed to need much sleep. He was always working at something—classes, sports, and part-time jobs. He was on the go all the time."

Dick loved football. By all accounts he was a very good player. He was solid, and quickly rose to become captain of the team. As a wrestler he didn't win the State Championships, but he came close. His third major sport was lacrosse, and it was here, while attending Colgate University, that he found himself face-to-face with future football legend Jim Brown, who played for Syracuse University.

"Dick never once backed down against the rushing strength of Jim Brown," said Bob Royer. "He held his own every game." Dick remembered those encounters differently: "I always wound up on my ass after an encounter with Jim Brown."

Jim Brown, named by Sporting News in 2002 as "the greatest professional football player ever," went on to another successful career as an actor.

* * *

Because of his athletic successes, in 2006 Dick was inducted into the McDonogh School Athletic Hall of Fame. He proudly attended the ceremony, accompanied by his wife, Bea, and daughter, Gina; cousin Mitzi and her children also attended. It was a wonderfully rewarding experience for the boy who didn't give a damn.

Bob Royer's father attended all of Dick's games. As an honorary member of the Royer family, Dick found himself in a foreign environment, one that was vastly improved over his own youthful life. Where he had dedicated his life to hurting and disappointing his own father, at this time all he wanted to do was to make Mr. Royer proud of him, with one exception.

The "I'm gonna fail just to hurt my father" demon still lingered within Dick Virgilio. It proved to be a difficult demon to exorcise.

By graduation time, Dick had risen to the rank of lieutenant at McDonogh, simply because he had learned so well how to play the game. He was far from an angel, but he knew how to work within the system and play his cards just right, to get away with things—little things just outside the area of acceptance by his superiors.

He wasn't a troublemaker, and perhaps that's why his shenanigans lasted as long as they did. Knowing where he had come from, and how hard he had worked fueled speculation that some McDonogh officials may have turned a blind eye at times.

But several weeks before Dick's graduation, that old demon surfaced from deep within.

"I decided I didn't want to be a lieutenant. That would have meant I had accomplished something. Having that officer's rank would have pleased my father too much. Or maybe I just didn't want the McDonogh experience to end.

"So, to spite my father, I went and did some crazy thing off campus and got caught. The school board busted me down to private. I remember distinctly thinking to myself, I'm going to do this, because I no longer have to play this game.

"Well, I got into big trouble. In retrospect, it was for nothing, because my parents were not at my graduation and probably never even knew that I got busted. I just ended up hurting a bunch of people who didn't deserve to be hurt."

Ironically, Dick had been doing better than ever before. He was captain of the football team, was invited into the personal homes of various teachers and coaches, and was given responsibility—trash truck routes, movie delivery, and screening.

Even his business on the side was doing extremely well—buying food and drink for the other students. This was his investment portfolio, things he did to financially increase his well being, and acts that earned him the respect of virtually the entire student body.

What was it then, that caused him to take such a serious step backward?

The most logical explanation for what turned his head was a letter he wrote home to his father around this time. In this letter, Dick, still hopeful that he could earn his father's love and respect, still searching for an "I love you" moment, painstakingly fought his dyslexia enough to construct a letter straight from his heart.

Sadly, his father mistook the dyslexia for stupidity. He took a red pen to it. He slashed his youngest son's letter apart with red edits designed to make the document bleed, and mailed it back to Dick.

Keep in mind, Dick hadn't seen his father since he ran away from home, but his father was scheduled to attend a major wrestling championship final, a match that Dick was expected to win handily.

The letter incident awoke such pain in Dick that his best friend, Bob Royer, still believes Dick may have undermined himself at the state wrestling championships.

"The question remains in the back of my mind, all these years later," Bob said, "that perhaps Dick knew he was good, knew he could have taken his opponent down that night. But I think he had one final resurgence of anger about his father and deliberately threw that match."

And, in Dick's own words, "Just like I submarined my hard-earned rank of lieutenant."

At that point, it wasn't just his own family, his own father, who suffered disappointment. His friends and teachers on campus were disappointed as well, including Mr. Royer and his wife, who were also in attendance that night.

All Dick could say about the match and his demotion was, "I just didn't want to be successful. I didn't want awards and accolades."

Dick, all these years later, still remembers the pain of the events leading up to his demotion.

"No one knew about my dyslexia, or the fears inside me every time I sat down to write something. The only thing that saved me year after year, and even through medical school, was my ability to memorize.

"Probably the only thing I could have been in life was a doctor, because a doctor can be dyslectic and it doesn't matter. Because all you do is memorize—what bone connected to what bone position. You can hide all that, and I was a master at hiding my disability.

"It took me forever to write that letter to my father."

"As I grew older it really hurt me, because I couldn't even write a note to my kids, or my wife, or write a letter. I still can't. But with the arrival of computers, I suddenly had spell check and grammar check to help me. I could see it on the screen, move things around, and make changes."

Today, Dick admits that, even with the use of the computer, it's still frustrating for him to attempt to write a letter. The only difference today, he said, is that he doesn't have a wastebasket filled with wadded up pieces of paper.

"It took me forever to write a one-page or two-page letter. It took me forever to write that letter to my father. And then he tore it apart in his own vile way and sent it back to me. And he probably took great delight in doing that.

"It crushed me, to be honest. And it really just confirmed the fact that my father was a dysfunctional jerk. I remember it was a very traumatic thing for me to write it.

"It was something I wanted to do. Deep down, I guess there was a part of me that still wanted to have a relationship with my father. I thought maybe a way to do that would be to write him a letter and say how sorry I was for running away. But that was my father. That was the way he operated with everyone around him. Apparently I was no exception."

The eventual graduation from military school in 1956 represented the most successful run in Dick Virgilio's life up to that point.

Between the years that have gone by, and his wounded and selective memory about his childhood, Dick himself cannot add much to this part of his life. Clearly, there was a lot of pain, and he has done a thorough job of concealing it, both from himself and from his family—of digging a hole and burying it.

Despite these contrasting personality traits, many others saw the potential in him. People liked him, trusted him, and were rooting for him to succeed. All the more disappointing to see him voluntarily go into the tank just before graduation.

Disappointment, however, was far from how Bob Royer described his friend:

"When I think of Dick Virgilio, I think of somebody who came in from the cold, who had a world of capability that he kept hidden under a bushel basket for a while, and once that basket was lifted off—and that started at McDonogh and ended at our farm and with my family—he began to mature into the great human being he is today.

"Dick is one of my real heroes in life. To be able to do all the things he's done, and with all the roadblocks thrown in front of him along the way, he is just amazing. When you start thinking about it, it's really quite mind-boggling."

Prom night 1956 at McDonogh.

SEVEN

The White Elephant

Neither of Dick's parents came to visit him at the military school. The only time he spoke to them after the runaway incident was many years later, after Dick and his family moved to San Diego, although there was a short time he visited them in Naples, Italy, where his father was stationed at the naval hospital as chief of surgery.

His parents were in Italy the day Dick graduated from McDonogh and apparently made no effort to attend. Only his mother's best friend was in attendance. That was it. No one else came. The friend worked for Uncle Frank and had been like an aunt to Dick — keeping track of his progress, his indiscretions, and no doubt reporting back to Uncle Frank with progress being made in Dick's life.

With McDonogh behind him, Dick Virgilio readied himself for college. He was a physically toned, street-smart product from the neighborhoods of Baltimore, honed by military-like training for five years. He brimmed with self-confidence, eager to see the world.

He had applied and been turned down by several schools, including William and Mary and the University of Virginia, but one major option remained, and it came from the most unlikely source — his father.

Dick's grades at McDonogh were good. Not great, but consistently good. They were good enough to get him into Colgate University as a legacy applicant.

"Legacy" meant that his father went there before him, which carried considerable weight for first-time applicants. Despite Dick's estrangement from his father, he knew this was a good opportunity for him—perhaps his only opportunity for moving forward.

For a short time he considered not attending Colgate, giving up his Naval Reserve status, and signing up for active duty. He knew that would really piss off his father, which in a warped sort of way made it even more appealing to him.

In the end, Dick decided to give Colgate a try and attempt to put a more positive spin on the next chapter of his life. It wouldn't be easy, but nothing was at that age.

At Colgate there was no more morning wake-up call, no trumpet-blaring reveille. No more trash emptying at first light. No marching around in perfectly pressed uniforms. And, best of all, Dick no longer had to salute his higher ups.

'Virgilio, what the hell's going on here?'

In college, Dick was virtually in charge of his own destiny. However, it appeared that this sudden lack of regimen, the absence of constant authority, caused him to slack considerably.

During his four years at Colgate, Dick's grades were far from enviable. In the first semester, fueled by his unchecked dyslexia and newly found freedom, he earned four F's and a D.

"I'll never forget that," Dick recalled. "The Dean called me in and said, 'Virgilio, what the hell's going on here?' Being the smart ass that I was, I told him I must have just spent too much time working to earn that D.

"Throughout my life, older Italian gentlemen have stepped in to steer me back on course. This fellow was no exception. He was as Italian as they get, and I think he felt sorry for me. He urged me to get my act together. And that began my crazy four years at Colgate

University, probably the most atypical college experience anyone ever had.

"I graduated with a 1.8 grade point average out of a possible 4.0. You can imagine how many D's and F's I would have had to get. But I graduated by once again learning how to play the system."

Colgate, located in Hamilton, New York, was in the wilderness of upstate New York, where the snowfall was measured in feet rather than in inches, and the temperature was in the single digits for much of the school year.

Still, Colgate University was, after all was said and done, a university. What was worse, it was a university of undisciplined young men.

Over the decades, such things as fraternity hijinks—class rivalries and initiations—became written off as "campus spirit." To address such mischief with any greater sincerity or attention went askew of the school's founding mission.

The school dates back to 1817, when 13 men founded the Baptist Education Society of the State of New York. "Thirteen dollars and thirteen prayers backed it," as the legend goes.

The institution's name was changed to the Hamilton Literary and Theological Institution, and, in 1846, to Madison University. The school would be renamed again in 1890 as Colgate, after an early founder, a soap maker named William Colgate. Today, young men and women attend side-by-side.

Andy Rooney, the Emmy-winning newsman and former host of CBS's "60 Minutes," is Colgate's most distinguished alumnus. Ed Werner and John Haney, the creators of the popular Trivial Pursuit game, also graduated from Colgate.

"Colgate is stuck in Hamilton, in the middle of nowhere," said Dick, shaking his head. "It's about thirty miles from Syracuse. At the time I attended Colgate, it was an all-male school. No women whatsoever. Talk about Animal House. And you couldn't drive anywhere in the winter because there was snow up to your rear-end.

"I didn't like it at all. I played football for my first and second years, but I wound up playing lacrosse all four years, and I really enjoyed it. But I realized I was not going to be good enough to accomplish anything in either of those sports. I also wrestled for two years. But athletics was not as important to me at Colgate, not as important as it had been at McDonogh.

"My major was math and my minor was biology. I chose biology because I became infatuated with taking cats and birds apart and seeing what made them tick.

"You don't have to be too creative, just know what's connected to what. You don't have to write a lot of essays about how a cat craps, or whatever. But, due to my dyslexia, I had to stay away from anything literary, or that had to do with writing.

Don't you ever lay a hand on me again!

"As a freshman, I found my way into Theta Chi, a big fraternity. It was the athletes' fraternity so we all rushed it. But it was so much BS. They had initiations where they paddled your ass. One day I grabbed the paddle from the guy paddling me, and I just about killed him with it. I said, 'Enough of this shit,' and I told him, 'Don't you ever lay a hand on me again!'

"They left us alone after that, but being part of the fraternity allowed me to work in the kitchen, so, essentially, I got free room and board. And I cleaned (I did a lot of cleaning at McDonogh, so it was second nature to me by then). It didn't cost anything to do that."

* * *

"There was a little town nearby called Canastota, where quite a large contingent of Italians had settled. One of the guys from school lived there. So one weekend I went home with him and somehow, in the middle of this huge Italian population of Canastota, I got to know the Bruno family.

"Dominic Bruno had two brothers, and together they owned everything. They owned a little restaurant and bar called The White

Elephant. They owned the vending machine franchise, which covered everything from candy to cigarettes. You name it, and they had it in a machine.

"It turned out that Dominic owned everything throughout the entire county. In Syracuse he owned the Three Rivers Inn, which was one of the largest and most popular nightclubs in that part of the country.

"I didn't realize it at the time, but Bruno was at the very center of Canastota and the region's well-connected organization of sucessful Italian businessmen.

Dominic Bruno took Dick into his family and mentored him for five years. He was Dick's personal Godfather and more than anyone else is responsible for his ultimately deciding to pursue a career in medicine. Bruno will always hold a special place in Dick's heart.

"Bruno and his family befriended me quickly. His sister was a neat gal, about 20 years older than me. She was a beautician, and she had a little place on the alley next to the White Elephant Restaurant. Tess was her name.

"I told Tess that I didn't have any money. I explained how my parents weren't sending me to college and weren't paying for anything. I told her how my uncle paid for the first semester, but that I was on my own now.

"She got it immediately that I was in pretty desperate shape and really needed to find a job to make some money and quick.

"She talked to Dominic, and he gave me a job washing dishes. Tess let me sleep in the back of her beauty salon, so I'd wash dishes until two in the morning, and then I'd crash in her beauty salon.

The White Elephant truck that Dick drove back and forth to Colgate University to advertise the nightclub. It was his sole form of transportation for those first three years of college, allowing him to work in Canastota 30 miles away, while still attending school at Colgate.

"Her daughter Sharon was a gorgeous gal. I would have loved to date her, but I never got up the nerve to ask her out. One night I mentioned to Tess that I didn't have any way to get back and forth from Colgate to Canastota—a thirty-mile jaunt each way. Again, she talked to her brother.

"So, I'm washing dishes one night and Dominic comes up to me and says, 'How'd you like another job?' I said, 'What's that?' He took me out and showed me this old delivery truck that he owned and literally standing upright in the truck bed was this enormous effigy of a white elephant. The truck screamed 'WHITE ELEPHANT,' on the doors, along with the address and phone number. It was the most obnoxious thing I had ever seen.

"Dominic said, 'I need to advertise a little more. And you need transportation. If you drive this truck to school, park it in front of your fraternity house, and drive it around, I'll pay you. Then you can come back here and wash dishes at night.' "

At this point it's not hard to visualize a strapping Dick Virgilio, muscles bursting out of his tight T-shirts and pants—this young Italian kid with good looks and an athlete's physique—driving in this god-awful old truck with an enormous white elephant climbing out of the truck bed. This was right out of the cartoons.

Yet, nobody had the nerve to give him a hard time. Dick had come of age, and he was not the sort of person one might make the butt of a joke. No, those days were long gone.

The White Elephant Night Club is where Dick began work as a dishwasher after starting college. It's where he met Dominic Bruno, the owner, who made him feel like family and ultimately influenced his decision to become a doctor.

"The guys at school couldn't believe it. One thing led to another and all of a sudden I wasn't washing dishes any more. I was busing tables. Then I was waiting tables. Next thing you know, I was tending bar in the White Elephant. And along the way I had become really good friends with Dominic, his wife, and his son, who was my age.

"Then, one day I realized, if I was gonna make this trip back and forth from work to school in this clown truck, I should probably take some stuff back and sell it. So, as I did for years at McDonogh, I started loading up the back of the truck with beer and other things I knew the guys would buy, and I drove up and down fraternity row selling it.

"I could put ten cases of beer in the rear of that old truck. And they were the big bottles, the quart bottles they used to sell in the stores. I obviously charged more than I paid for them, so I made a lot of money on the side.

Dominic greeting movie star Peter Lawford upon his arrival at the Three Rivers Inn.

"One day I approached Dominic and asked him if he ever thought about putting his vending machines on campus? I explained how college kids were always looking for snacks and this and that.

"Dominic said, 'I've never thought of that. Do you think you can get them in?' 'No Problem,' I said. And that was the beginning of yet another moneymaking scheme I came up with to make school more fun, or at least tolerable.

"Dominic's brother would drive this truckload of machines down to Colgate University, and I'd go from fraternity house to fraternity house, selling them on the concept. 'Look what you can have here,' I said. 'Candy, cigarettes, you name it.' So, sure as hell, they all wanted vending machines.

"I always had a deal going, and always had a wad of cash in my pocket."

"Once or twice a week I'd have to restock the machines and take

The Three Rivers Inn was a large nightclub and lounge located in Syracuse. This is where Dick learned all aspects of the nightclub business. He recalls spending hours behind this bar and in the large adjacent showroom waiting tables. The club hosted entertainers such as Nat King Cole, Bobby Darin, Connie Francis and many others. To this day Dick swears that he made more money waiting tables and bartending at the Three Rivers Inn than he did in his first five years as a doctor.

the money back to Dominic. I don't know how I even got a 1.8 grade point average, to tell you the truth, what with how hard I was working on the side.

"I always had a deal going, and always had a wad of cash in my pocket. I'd buy the beer for 50 cents and I'd bring it back and sell it for a dollar. College kids. They didn't care. So I'd make a profit on the stuff I brought over, plus I got a percentage of the vending machine profits. I had never made so much money.

"I never once thought about cheating Dominic. This guy was my idol. I loved him and would do anything for him, or for his sister, or for his entire family for that matter. On weekends I'd go to his house for family meals—big pasta dinners. I was treated like one of the family."

One night after dinner, Dominic sat down with Dick and they began to discuss all the deals Dick had going on. Dominic was like a proud father as he sat there and listened. Then he suggested that Dick should have a car of his own.

Dick looked quizzically at Dominic, as the Godfather of this old Italian family explained that he knew people, and asked how much money Dick had. Before the evening ended, Dick had given Dominic a handful of bills, entrusting him to find what essentially would become Dick's first car.

In a short amount of time, Dominic presented Dick with a 1956 Ford convertible.

"Oh, it was a beautiful car. It had the sexy round taillights and fins in the rear. It was red with black trim and smothered in chrome.

"I would still drive the truck for advertising purposes, but I had a nice ride to go out in when I wanted to."

* * *

In the summers, Dick had no reason to leave New York because he was working full-time in Canastota. One day a policeman mentioned to Dick they were looking for cops on the Canastota police force—a small group of dedicated policemen who basically just kept peace in the town.

Dick met the police chief and before he knew it he was talked into being a part-time Canastota police officer.

"The chief asked if I had ever fired a gun. I told him I had shot a few squirrels as a kid. He said nothing ever happens in Canastota, so I became a part-time cop."

Originally called Kniste Stota, from an Oneida Nation Indian name meaning "cluster of pines near still waters," Canastota is a small onion-growing village located along the banks of the Erie Canal. It now hosts the International Boxing Hall of Fame.

This Three Rivers entertainment flyer from 1962 demonstrates a typical year at the Inn.

As Canastota's newly sworn official, Dick drove a police car, wore a badge, toted a gun, and wore a policeman's uniform, and to this day he swears he had more than one bullet, making light of TV's Barney Fife and Mayberry RFD.

"You know, all that time, I never once thought about what I was gonna do if I had to pull my gun. It was just a peaceful little place. I got to know all the Italian families. I was invited to nearly every Italian home in town for dinner at one time or another. I was never more proud of my Italian heritage."

Dick would visit Canastota years later, when his daughter Gina graduated from Colgate University. Gina became the third generation Virgilio to attend and graduate.

"I just loved Canastota. Everybody's name ended in a vowel, we were all good friends; I was happy. And then I was asked by Dominic to work in his nightclub, the Three Rivers Inn, in Syracuse. That was a major promotion for me.

"It was closed in the winter, but was a busy hot spot the rest of the year. I waited tables and tended bar. On a busy night I could make up to $500 in tips.

"They had a dock out front, and while I was there we built a hotel and I worked construction. I wore a hard hat, poured cement, and at night I was a waiter or bartender. As a reward for my hard work and loyalty, I was given a permanent room in the hotel that I helped build.

"Dominic brought in big acts. He had Nat King Cole, Bobby Darren, and Connie Francis. You name it, of who was popular in those days, and they all performed at the Three Rivers Inn.

"I worked various jobs there, wherever they needed me. I was bartender, waiter, and maître d'. I can't tell you how much money I was making back then, but my pockets were always full with cash.

"We wore tuxedo pants and red jackets when waiting and bartending, and a cummerbund. As the maître d' I wore a suit, or at least a sport coat. It was a high-class operation.

"All of the big wheeler-dealers in Syracuse would come out to the night club, especially with the big stars we had performing there.

"All summer and part of the winters I stayed in the hotel room Dom gave me. It became my own private room. Sometimes we would close down during the winter, but we had a boat at the dock, and, on mild winter days, I would run that for Dom as well. What a time that was.

If it meant getting a woman for
Nat King Cole, that was my job.

"When the stars came in, Dom would say, 'Don't bother me with the stars and their needs. Whatever they want, you take care of it.'

"If it meant getting a woman for Nat King Cole, that was my job; if it meant escorting a female fan up to Bobby Darren's room, that was my job too. If I had to run out at all hours for a peanut butter-and-jelly sandwich for Connie Francis, that's what I did.

"And I was getting tips like crazy. Waiting on tables, bartending, working as maître d', driving the boat—all this put tips in my pocket—lots of tips.

* * *

During this time, Dick somehow graduated from Colgate, in spite of his bad grades. It was 1960 and Dick was 22 years old.

"I finished up at Colgate University and stayed consistent with my crappy 1.8 grade point average. Not that I cared, but I knew I wasn't going to get into any good schools, certainly not into medical school. My grades were so bad I really don't know how they could have graduated me. Maybe they were just glad to get rid of me."

As with McDonogh, nobody came to see him at his graduation at Colgate. "In fact, I don't even think I was there," Dick said with a laugh, retelling the story years later. However, the day Dick graduated, there may have been a lot of underclassmen wearing black armbands. Nobody ever did the things he did for his fellow classmates.

"After graduating from Colgate, I told Dominic that I was there with him for good. He pulled me aside and said he wanted to give me some advice. 'You can take it or not,' he said. 'Are you sure you want to do this? You know I love you like a son. You've always worked hard for me—harder than my own son, Ron. But he is my son, and he's going to get all of this one day.'

"Dom painted the picture for me, that in ten years I would

probably still be making a lot of money, and having this exciting life-style, but I would always be just a waiter or bartender, or go-to guy for the boss. 'This business will never be yours,' he said.

"For Dominic to sit me down and give me that advice was beyond anything I expected or hoped for. I loved Dominic. I trusted him. So, at that point he had my attention, and I started thinking that maybe I had really made a mistake with my life. Maybe it was time to see what I could do to change things around."

The Godfather of Canastota had more to say. Dick sat motionless listening to every word.

"You're always welcome here," Dominic said. "As long as I have a business, you have a job. But that's all it's ever going to be . . . a job."

Dick had told Dominic about his father and uncle being doctors, and how much he was attracted to that field. The human body fascinated him. He loved his time in biology, dissecting small animals. He knew deep down that he wanted to be a doctor.

"Dominic asked me if I had any other ambitions I wanted to pursue, and he specifically mentioned the field of medicine. Dominic was a powerful man. He asked me, is there any chance at all I could get into medical school. I told him I didn't think so."

But Dick had mentioned earlier to Dominic that he had an uncle who was a prominent doctor in Baltimore, who had helped him out years before when he was a runaway.

"Dominic told me not to hurt myself in the long run, that I would end up kicking myself if I missed this opportunity because of some silly resentment for my father.

"He said it was time for me to take charge of my life and make a success of it, and stop trying to disappoint my father. I realized he was absolutely right, so I went to see my Uncle Frank again."

EIGHT

Medical School

Son, this world is rough
And if a man's gonna make it, he's gotta be tough
So I give ya that name and I said goodbye
I knew you'd have to get tough or die
And it's the name that helped to make you strong.
—Johnny Cash ("A Boy Named Sue")

Whether Dick was willing to admit it or not, like the song lyric, his father's cold and loveless approach to fatherhood contributed to his toughness.

Dick's journey to get to this point in life wasn't easy, but a lesser man might not have survived at all. If it had been the school of hard knocks, Dick would have gotten a 4.0 grade point average.

Throughout his life that same resilience, that refusal to give up, reared its head again and again. It served him from those early days when he ran away from home. It got him through his military school trials, through college, through medical school, through Vietnam, and through numerous life-threatening medical setbacks.

Was it in his DNA, in his genes, to be a doctor? Possibly. But to cross that bridge Dick had to demonstrate a determination to his Uncle Frank as sincere and convincing as he had ever felt. He wanted

Dick's beloved Uncle Frank. Were it not for his support and help who knows what would have happened to the 13-year-old runaway.

deep down to be a doctor, but would Uncle Frank invest in such an ambition?

"I hadn't seen Uncle Frank for some time, but I made a trip down to Baltimore to visit him in 1961. After I told him my story, he looked down at me from his big, ornate desk, and said, 'You've got to be shitting me. After all this, you're twenty-two years old, and *now* you tell me you want to be a doctor?'

"When I told him I had been out of college for a year, he asked what I had been doing. I was reluctant to tell him everything, but I assured him I didn't have to ask anybody for money, that I wasn't on the dole. I was self-sufficient and a college graduate—barely, mind you, but a college graduate just the same. I wanted to be a doctor.

"I'll make you proud."

"I asked Uncle Frank if he could help me get accepted into a medical school. He looked at me like I was crazy. I told him that my performance at Colgate (my 1.8 GPA) didn't reflect my true intellect, that I had crappy grades not because I was stupid, but because I didn't care. I was busy making a living and doing other things. I pointed out that those things were going to make me a better person in my life.

"I did work a lot of jobs, and worked hard; I organized and figured ways to get along without having to beg for anything. I danced around my handicaps. No matter what it was, I got it done. I just told him how it was—that I felt really good about that part of me. I did my best to convince him that I didn't feel it was a wasted five or six years, and that I could do this. I knew I had the IQ; I just never applied myself.

"Uncle Frank looked at me and just shook his head. I imagine he was thinking, 'Jesus, I'm gonna have to call in some favors, and this little shit is gonna let me down.' But I told him again, 'I'll never let you down. If you can help me, I'll make you proud.'"

Ironically, that was not a conversation Dick could have had with his uncle any time earlier. But the timing was right.

Uncle Frank sent him on a mission to obtain various documents and forms he would need to approach the medical school board. Dick returned to Syracuse and his job working for Dominic.

* * *

"It was several months after my meeting with Uncle Frank that I received a letter from the dean at the University of Maryland Medical School inviting me down for an interview. About that same time I got a one-line note from Uncle Frank that simply said, 'Don't make me regret this.'

"I'll never forget that first meeting with Dean Stone. He was furious that he had to admit a student to his medical school with such pitiable records. He was obviously not happy, and said, 'Let me tell you something son . . .' So, I'm thinking this guy is a real prick, but I looked him in the eye and said, 'Yes, sir?'

"You're not going to last six months here."

"He looked up from the paperwork and said, 'I've got to do this, and I'm not happy about it. We want you to join the class of 1965, University of Maryland Medical School. Your classes begin in September, but I can tell you this much, you're not going to last six months here.'

"I looked at him and said, 'Well, thank you very much. I'll be here in September, and we'll just have to see how long I last.' "

The dean obviously didn't know the man to whom he was talking. He had some transcripts and educational records in front of him on paper, and he had a request from an important man in the community he couldn't ignore (perhaps that's what irritated him the most). But he completely underestimated the tough little Italian kid sitting in front of him.

"He had no idea how motivated I was to do well, and how that motivation would result in me being one of the top students in the Class of 1965 at his precious medical school.

"That was the point when I no longer cared what my father wanted. I knew what I wanted, and I wasn't going to continue to screw around in Syracuse any longer.

"Once I was in medical school, there was no turning back. I was committed. I could see clearly the path in front of me for the first time in my life. I wanted to be the best medical student and the best doctor who ever lived. I worked my ass off to reach that goal. And I never looked back after that."

This was a huge decision for Dick, and he was more than a little nervous, but he returned to Syracuse to say his goodbyes. Soon afterward, he found a room in the Baltimore student dormitory and moved in his few possessions. He didn't know a soul. He had a lot of money in his pocket and a shiny Ford Fairlane convertible parked outside, but that was it.

"The first day of orientation I realized I was a couple years older than most of these students, who had graduated top of their class from college, and got into medical school legitimately. I sat there, looking around, and I had this great epiphany. I suddenly realized, good God, if I can't compete with these idiots, I'm in trouble.

"From then on I valued medical school. It wasn't hard for me. Actually, I found medical school easy, because I loved every minute of it, every aspect of it. I had picked up certain people skills working for Dominic Bruno, and my confidence was high. I'd learned to work around my dyslexia so it no longer kept me from doing well.

"I still remember my first cadaver. We had a big laboratory where the bodies were on tables and two people were assigned to each cadaver. You would go to the lecture hall and the professor might announce that today we would be working on the brain. After a thorough lecture on the brain, we would spend all day sitting there with the formaldehyde and the cadaver. Your eyes would water and everybody had a special name for their cadaver. I think mine was 'Oscar.' "

✳ ✳ ✳

"When I graduated from there, four years later, that same Dean, the one who told me I wouldn't last six months, had to present me cum laude, Alpha Omega Alpha Honors, and a slew of other medical and surgical awards. He had to announce my name and list each of the awards, and then he had to shake my hand. I remember that moment well. I just looked at him.

"I know how you're doing, and I'm proud of you."

"My Uncle Frank, God Bless him, died six months before I graduated. But he knew he made a good investment in me. He died of pancreatic cancer. Fortunately, I went to his house before he died. Cousin Mitzi showed me in, and I kneeled next to his bed. I said, 'Uncle Frank, I wanna thank you for everything you've done for me.' I said, 'I want you to know how I'm doing.' He stopped me mid-sentence and said, 'I know how you're doing, and I'm proud of you Dick.'

"That was a heart-wrenching moment for me, to hear him say those words. That was the greatest validation a young man could ever hope to hear.

"I was hoping he would live long enough to attend my graduation, but that wasn't meant to be. I was fortunate in so many regards, and it was very special to him, and to me, that he got to live long enough to see me turn my life around.

"You take the Uncle Franks and Dominic Brunos out of the picture, and I don't get out. I may be in jail. But I'm not a doctor. Throughout my entire life, all those years, all that money and time he invested, it had finally paid off, in his eyes."

The "King of Baltimore" was how Dick referred to his Uncle Frank. He was a very prominent Italian surgeon who had bought acres of real estate, shopping centers, etc. He made heaps of money and dabbled in politics. He was the Parks Commissioner. Frank Marino was benevolent to a fault, and donated to numerous institutions, which may explain his pull both at the military school and medical school.

Dick's cousin Mitzi, who, even to this day, probably doesn't realize how much weekly outings to her home meant to a troubled 9-year-old.

In a way, Dick was the son Frank Marino never had. Frank's other nephews, from his brothers' families, "were all bad guys," as Dick would describe them years later. And Dick's older brother was not close to Uncle Frank in the least, which made Dick Virgilio very fortunate indeed.

"Despite Uncle Frank's long history of generosity, and how he helped my mother all those years, I think the first time I had a real conversation with him   the first time we really had a man-to-man talk   was that day I went to his office and asked him to help me get into medical school.

"Think about it. He got me out of California when I ran away. He took care of my mother her entire life. He got me into military school. He helped me get in the front door at medical school.

"It's not like I went to his house every weekend when I was a kid. I didn't see him that much. He had a cottage in Ocean City, Maryland, (and his daughter still has it). Once in awhile my mother and I would go there, but I never really had an honest-to-God conversation with him, a serious conversation with him, until that day in his office.

"After that I would see him often, and we would have dinner together. We would talk about the school (which was his medical school, too) and once or twice a month we would get together, especially if my mother was in town, which was infrequent. A day doesn't go by I don't think of my Uncle Frank and how he was there for me at every juncture in my life."

* * *

During his time at Colgate, Dick had remained in the Navy Reserve and continued to do weekly duty at night. They were usually four-to-six-hour courses. During his first two summers at Colgate, he performed submarine duty.

"When I went to medical school, I joined what they called the Ensign 1999 Program, where, as a medical student, you could continue your reserve time but had to spend two months every summer as an extern at a naval hospital. And that turned out to be fortuitous as well."

NINE

Bea

Beatrice Leona Strollo was the third of four sisters from a proud Italian family. Born and raised in Barnesboro, Pennsylvania, Bea and her two older sisters were born at home. Her sister-in-law was a nurse and assisted as midwife on the first deliveries, and may have served as an inspiration for young Bea.

"My first memory of Dick was when I was introduced to him at the Bachelor Officer Quarters in Bethesda, Maryland," recalled Bea. "I was sitting on the couch and someone said, 'This is Dick Virgilio.'

"I'll never forget. That first day he was wearing a plaid, short-sleeve shirt with the shirttail hanging out. It had a white background with blue and green stripes going through it. He used to wear his shirttails hanging out all the time.

"When I first saw him, I thought, gee, he's a big guy, but I thought he was pretty cute. My mother thought he was cute, too, until she found out he wanted to be a doctor. She was not happy about that doctor business.

"Dick had a roommate named Dan. So our first date was a double date. My girlfriend Nola was with Dick, and I was with Dan. We went over to Baltimore's Little Italy because there was a carnival going on."

It was love at first sight for Dick when he met Bea, and, shy as he

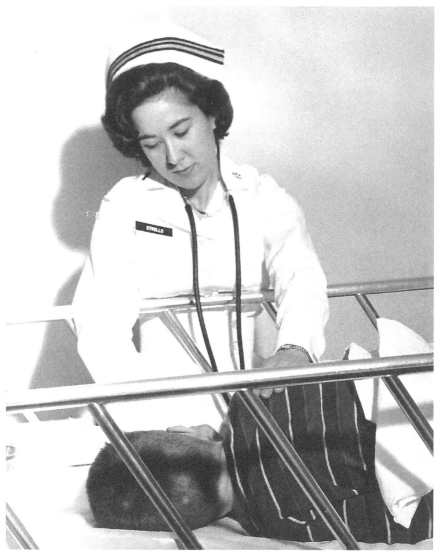

Nurse Bea, in 1965, just after Dick and Bea had gotten married. This was taken at Bethesda Naval Hospital.

was, he let his roommate Dan talk them into that double date. Trouble was, Dick got the wrong girl.

"I was never a ladies' man. I always felt inferior—couldn't dance worth a crap, and I was definitely a wallflower as it related to dating and stuff like that."

By then Dick had sold his beloved Ford convertible and bought a smaller Fiat, so everyone sat close together.

"It was like a little blue box," said Bea.

During that first double date, Bea and Dan were in the back seat and Dick was driving.

"All I could do was watch in the rearview mirror," Dick said, "and I couldn't stop looking at Bea."

What he didn't see, or remember seeing, was Dan trying to get Bea to kiss him the entire date. Years later, in the retelling of this story, Bea insisted Dan meant nothing to her, and recalled that her date that night with Dan could actually be summed up in one word, "creepy."

Meanwhile, in the front seat, Dick didn't want to be with Nola at all, and couldn't stop staring at Bea in the rearview mirror. All he could think about was how much he wanted to be with this beautiful Italian girl, to take her out and be alone with her.

"I just decided then and there I wanted to have my kids with her."

"I remember clearly when I first saw Bea. I thought, hey, I've just got to go out with that girl. I was really attracted to her, and I loved that she was Italian.

"Right away I knew I had a thing for her, and I usually wasn't like that with other girls. I didn't date a lot and didn't, you know. But it was funny, because Danny wound up with her in the back seat. And I'm up here in the front seat with this clown Nola, and I didn't like that at all.

"Bea was just so cute and so Italian; I enjoyed that she had a medical background as a nurse and I just decided then and there I wanted to have my kids with her. I don't know what came over me; I mean it was crazy. And of course, at that time, I was just beginning to get over this issue with my father."

For the first time in Dick's life he didn't feel haunted by his father's looming shadow.

When Dick and Bea first met, she was a navy nurse, working at the Bethesda Naval Hospital in the Washington, D.C., area, where Dick was externing. As externs, the medical personal stayed in the Bachelor Officer Quarters—one wing for men and one wing for women—not officially residing at the institution.

While Dick had been out with Bea once, he was still quite shy. He knew she got off work at 11 p.m., so he sat on the steps of the BOQ, for several nights, waiting for her to walk by. Before a week had passed, Dick asked Bea out on a date, just the two of them. He took her out for burgers.

"We would go down and have little White Castle hamburgers," said Bea. "They were small, thin, with little chopped up pickles on them. They were so delicious. Dick would have twelve, and I'd have two."

They began dating regularly. Dick never dated another woman after that.

"When we first met, he had an awful temper," said Bea. "I almost broke up with him because he would get so upset if I would forget about our date. My dad had passed away, so I'd go see my mother periodically. I'd come back and he would yell, 'We had a date!' I'd deny it, of course, and he would get so upset. Finally, I just said, 'Hey, I don't need this.' He finally shaped up," she said and laughed.

"The other thing that really bugged me was that he always had a habit of looking at his watch. Finally, I just said, 'Hey, do you wanna be out with me or home looking at your watch?'"

Dick later defended that as just a nervous habit, but the memory still makes them both laugh.

Soon he found an apartment in Baltimore's Little Italy. He wanted to get back to his Italian roots, so he moved into a row house there, above an Italian restaurant, and just big enough for Dick and his roommate.

As an ensign, Dick received minimal extern pay. He spent most of his time following doctors around, watching their procedures, or working in the animal lab or the research lab. That lasted throughout the summer months, until he returned to medical school.

Eventually, about six months after they started dating, Dick invited Bea to the Royer's farm for the first time.

"I think I knew the Royers long before I had ever met Dick's own parents," said Bea. "We would have a ball out there. We did a lot of horseback riding. They had a big German shepherd I was deathly afraid of, but we would spend weekends out there together."

* * *

Dick had committed himself to becoming a doctor. For the first time in his life he began to realize how brief life really was. He was in love and wanted to get on with things—things like a career, marriage to Bea, and starting a family. Part of that process meant introducing Bea to his mother and father.

"You can't marry that girl. She's too short."

"My father and mother lived in Washington, D.C. He was stationed at the Naval Station, and I took Bea to meet them during our second year together.

"I was so proud of her, and I wanted her to meet my parents. Wouldn't you know it, my father pulled me aside and said, 'You can't marry that girl. She's too short.' This was coming from a man who was barely five feet tall. I swear to God, I couldn't believe my own ears."

Bea's father died when she was 12. Once Dick was sure that Bea would say yes to a proposal, he asked her mother for Bea's hand in marriage. The future mother-in-law looked at him and, in no uncertain terms, explained the rules to Dick.

"You can marry my daughter," she said, "as long as you don't become a doctor. I don't trust doctors."

Bea's mother blamed doctors for her husband's death. Dick explained to her that he had invested a lot of time and effort in his quest to become a doctor, and it was too late to change professions. Eventually she relented and gave the young couple her blessing. But, until the day she died, at 99, she never missed an opportunity to let Dick know how much she disliked doctors.

All of this points up why the Royer family was so special not only to Dick, but to Bea. There was a parental normalcy there that was lacking elsewhere in their lives.

Dick tells a funny story about Bea and her car. "Bea was from a little coal mining town up in Pennsylvania and drove around in this big Chevy four-door thing. She could barely see over the steering wheel.

"One day we were going up to the Royer's farm for a New Year's Eve party and Bea drove. We got a flat tire and she says, 'No problem. I've got a lot of tires in the trunk.' So I open the trunk and there must have been 15 tires in there, but no rims. Turns out she was buying them wherever she saw tires for sale—the Goodwill or whatever—but didn't realize they had to be on rims.

"Well, I'm afraid that I got pretty upset at that. Here we were, in the dead of winter, at night, and in the middle of nowhere, with an unfixable flat tire. Ha ha ha. Somehow, we hitched a ride to the Royers, and now we both laugh at the retelling of that story."

The years between 1962 and 1965 were good years. Dick moved forward with his medical education like a man on a mission. He was happier than ever before because Bea was in his life. "The Sixties" were unfolding around them—an era of rock 'n' roll and free love—but they were locked in a bubble of their own love, and that's all that mattered.

In September, Dick returned to medical school in Baltimore and Bea continued her work as a navy nurse at Bethesda in post-op open-heart surgery. It wasn't too far to drive from Bethesda to the University of Maryland—maybe 35 miles—so Dick visited Bea a lot. And she drove to see him as well. At about this time, they started spending weekends at the Royer's farm.

"I was amazed that Dick never studied on weekends," said Bea. "But he learned by hearing."

Dr. and Mrs. Richard Virgilio.

The dyslexia had taught Dick new ways to learn. Dick explained, "I didn't take notes in classes or lectures, because I couldn't read my own handwriting. It was so hard to read, I just thought, why take them? I would memorize everything, and that's how I did so well."

Dick had finished his first year of medical school by the time he met Bea.

"In those days you had one or two patients in the little cardiac

Mr. Royer acting father of the bride.

unit, and they would only be in for three-to-five days, and then go to the ward. So Dick would come up on weekends to see me," said Bea.

"Yeah, I really wanted to see her," Dick said, "but the fact that she was working in that unit was also very exciting to me, because it gave me a chance to see how they took care of heart patients, and that was the sort of thing I was really interested in learning more about."

Since Dick was a medical student, the chief nurse didn't seem to mind him tagging along.

Dick and Bea on the way to their wedding reception, June 1965.

"Dick was always enthusiastic about medicine and surgery," said Bea. "He just loved it and never seemed to get enough.

"Doctor McClenathon was a big cheese in the navy during this time. He was one of the military pioneers in cardiac surgery and was very well known at the time," she said. "Dick thought a lot of him, and actually wanted to be a thoracic surgeon. But he went to Vietnam instead."

As time went by, Dick and Bea began to talk about more of a commitment, about getting married and having a family.

"It really bugged me," said Bea. "We dated three years before we got married. He was waiting, quote unquote, for his older brother to get married first. His brother finally got engaged, so we got engaged, too. But Dick kept stalling and stalling, waiting for his brother to tie the knot, which he never did.

"One weekend out on the Royer farm I told Mrs. Royer how ridiculous it all was—three years going together, and I was beginning to wonder if something was happening here or not. Mrs. Royer said, 'Well, you better tell him that.' So I did. I just told him, 'I'm not waiting any longer.' During Christmas he finally proposed, and we were married in June."

As usual, the Royers were a voice of reason in their young lives.

"Mr. Royer gave me away at our wedding," said Bea. "None of their kids were at the farm when we started going there together, so we had the place all to ourselves. It was really wonderful, and we did that almost every other weekend. The Royers were really special people."

"We actually fixed up their son Bob with two or three dates. He finally married one of them. Joanne, and she's a real doll, just really gorgeous.

"Dick and I were married in Kensington, Maryland, at the Catholic church next to Bethesda Naval Hospital. We tied the knot on June 12, 1965. I was a lieutenant and upon graduation, Dick had also finally become a lieutenant."

Dick had to remain an ensign throughout his time in medical school because of the Ensign 19 programs. Meanwhile, Bea became a lieutenant, j.g., then a full lieutenant. So, until he graduated at the rank of lieutenant, Bea frequently enjoyed pulling rank on him.

As their wedding date grew near, Dick became more and more excited about building the perfect honeymoon. Nothing would be too good for his new bride. He began to lay out the plan.

"As we were preparing for our marriage, I go to visit this travel agent in Bethesda. I tell him we are getting married June twelfth, and that we want a honeymoon, a special honeymoon. He immediately suggests that we go to the Bahamas. 'Everybody on the east coast goes to the Bahamas for their honeymoon,' he tells me.

"I said that would be great, but I wanted a nice hotel, too. The travel agent explained that we would be staying at the Grand Bahama Hotel and flying into Nassau the day after our wedding. 'We'll get you a room here the night before, and then you and Bea can fly out the next day,' he said. Oh, and he promised he would have a nice car, a convertible, waiting for us.

"So we get married and the next day we fly down to Nassau for this wonderful honeymoon. We get to the airport, go through customs, and I pick up our convertible. Then the fellow asks me what hotel we're staying at. I reach in my pocket for the information and proudly exclaim that we're staying at the Grand Bahama Hotel.

"He looks me like I'm crazy, so I asked what the problem was. 'You want to know what's the matter?' he asked. 'This is a very nice car you have here, state of the art and lots of extras, but it doesn't have pontoons, and your hotel is about 100 miles north of here, over the water.'

"Well, at that point I didn't know what to do. My travel agent had booked us on a different island than we were flying in to. It was June, and that time of year everything in Nassau was booked solid. So there we were, Bea and I, newlyweds, driving around Nassau in our beautiful new, 1965 Chevy convertible, with no place to stay.

"The only thing we could do was to go to a different hotel each night, sit in the lobby, and wait, and hope someone didn't show up for their reservation. As it turns out, we stayed in a bunch of different hotels, waking early to pack our stuff and move to the next.

"I felt like a complete idiot. To this day, when Bea disagrees with something I'm about to do she reminds me, 'Hey, you took care of the honeymoon, right?'

"When we got home I went down to that travel office, and they had closed up shop—out of business. The good news is that somehow, during all of this hotel swapping, Bea managed to get pregnant."

Maria, their first child, was born nine months later, March 24, 1966.

"Six months into my first pregnancy I had to resign from the navy," said Bea. "I wore sweaters and tried to hide it, but one day the chief nurse called me in and said, 'Now, Mrs. Virgilio, when were you going to tell us about your condition?'" In the 1960s, expectant naval officers were required to resign. Nowadays they can have their babies and remain on active duty, but in 1965 Bea had no choice. She had to leave her career in the navy and become a stay-at-home-mother.

When Maria was born, Dick was interning. He left for Vietnam in July, when his daughter was only three months old. It goes without saying that Bea wasn't real happy about the fact that he volunteered for Vietnam.

"I felt duty bound to go to Vietnam because I knew I could contribute in helping care for the young men who were being injured. I knew they needed good medical attention, and I was determined to be part of that. But leaving Bea and my first child was, without a doubt, one of the hardest things I ever had to do."

TEN

Vietnam

The year Dick and Bea married, 1965, the United States' involvement in Vietnam had grown to 200,000 personnel. American planes were conducting nearly continuous air raids, and heavy fighting was taking place on the ground. As more and more troops were deployed to Vietnam, the need for medical aid grew exponentially.

By then, Dick was considered a competent navy physician. As news filtered back to this country about Vietnam, like most young doctors, Dick wanted to be a part of that operation. He wanted to be there, where the action was, applying his newly obtained skills to helping our wounded soldiers.

"After I did my surgical internship in Bethesda, I signed up for Vietnam. It was a tough decision to make because I didn't have to go. I volunteered. But I agonized over that decision for a long time.

"I had this burning loyalty to my country, and while I didn't know the politics of the war in Vietnam, I knew that guys were dying over there, and this was what I had been trained for. I believed I could make a difference by helping our wounded soldiers.

"I had stayed in Bethesda after medical school to do my surgical internship. Maria was born March 24th, and by July 4th I was gone on a thirteen-month deployment.

"I know it was hard on Bea. She couldn't understand why in the world I would do that. I explained as best I could that they needed help, and I felt I had the gift. I believed I could make a difference.

"I knew that when Maria grew up, she would be proud of me if she knew that I went over to help all those young men getting shot in battle. Still, my wanting to leave her and travel into harm's way half way around the world was difficult for Bea to understand. I anguished over it and had many sleepless nights.

"To make matters worse, Bea was pregnant with our second child when I left, but neither of us knew it at the time. This OB/GYN friend of mine assured me that Bea couldn't get pregnant when she was nursing. Well, obviously that was not true, but like I say, I didn't know she was pregnant again for quite some time later.

"Leading up to my departure, I was working twenty hours a day, seven days a week, so I didn't really get a chance to see Maria a lot before I left.

"I'll never forget going down to Dulles Airport that day, with Bea carrying little Maria, and me knowing she was going to return to the house alone, in a strange and new neighborhood. There were all kinds of thoughts going through my mind: Did I do the right thing? Should I have delayed and gone later? Would Bea and Maria be all right?

"Before I left I made sure I was going to get orders to a hospital—to a MASH unit hospital—where I would actually be operating on people and putting my training to the best possible use. The navy had just opened a hospital in Da Nang. When I said I would volunteer, they said, 'Shit, we'll send you wherever you want to go.' Most of the people over there were drafted.

"Just like my father did before me."

"I always wanted to cut and sew, and be a surgeon, which sort of unsettled me because it went against my feelings for my father, who was a cut-and-sew surgeon.

"I was very conflicted about the whole thing. Yet, here I was, following in his damned footsteps. Here I was, in the navy. Here I was, going to war . . . just like my father did before me."

Dick had to fly into Clark Air Force Base in the Philippines to change planes. He had an overnight layover, so he booked himself into the Bachelor Officers' Quarters and left his luggage, except for a shaving kit and the clothes he was wearing, at the airport.

About six in the morning he heard a knock at the door and was greeted by a friendly Filipino girl claiming she was there to do his laundry. Dick, reeling from an emotional and lengthy flight, surrendered all his clothes to her with the promise that she would bring them back in two hours. He never saw her or the clothes again. Fortunately, the desk sergeant at the BOQ had some spare clothing.

Finally, he arrived in Da Nang. Trauma surgery was not his field, although he had done some training in that area. Dick quickly realized he was not only the least trained of the men in his MASH unit, but he was the youngest—a young, volunteer, trainee surgeon fresh out of his surgical internship.

"Once I got to Da Nang, it was total immersion. I mean, within minutes you were busy. You didn't have time to think about babies and wives and what you were—what you left behind and everything. You were busy all the time. Night, day, there was no end to it.

"Transitional shock aside, it was a very rewarding experience for me in the sense that I was able to help a tremendous amount of people with complete focus, and in a very short amount of time.

"There was no time to worry about the things that you usually worried about in civilian life: Is the traffic going to be tough going home? Are the bills going to get paid? Things like, how much is this piece of equipment, how much should I charge this guy? Is my office overhead too high? I was solely focused on one thing, and one thing only—cutting, sewing, and taking care of injured people.

"The hard part was being the youngest guy there. I had to do a lot of the crap jobs. If I was available, I took care of all the Vietnamese casualties, both civilian and military. This included a significant number of POWs—captured NVA (North Vietnamese Army) and Viet Cong."

* * *

Triage is defined as the process of deciding which patients should be treated first, based on how seriously injured they are or what their chances of survival might be. Needless to say, triage was a major component of Dick's job.

"You would hear the incoming helicopters, their blades thumping a loud 'boom boom boom.' Then, all of a sudden you'd have fifteen guys lined up in triage. Well, we only had four operating rooms, so somebody has to decide who goes and who doesn't—what the priority and criteria are, who has the best chance of surviving.

"Not all of these people were going to survive. A lot of them could've survived if we had gotten to them in time, but with only four operating rooms, you can only do four cases at a time. Someone has to make the tough decisions, 'Okay, 1-2-3-4, these guys go first.' Then, '5-6-7-8, these guys go second,' and right on down the line.

"Many times you would leave the triage area where a patient was getting fluids, blood, and temporary treatment. You would have to go to the operating room to work on more critical cases. Then, when you came out, he'd be dead.

"There were times when I just didn't know whether or not I made the right decision, because the guy you took might die on the operating table. And the guy you didn't select for surgery died, too. The corpsman points and tells you, 'Well, he's in the morgue. He's in the morgue. And he's in the morgue, too.'

"Mentally that was very hard for me. I got used to it after a while. Not to be disrespectful, but, in fact, it got . . . sullenly humorous, for lack of a better description, and that morbid sense of humor resulting from such a stressful form of work helped us get through the day.

"In medicine, when you're dealing with life and death, and you see so much destruction, and so much death hour after hour, you begin to joke about it. Making light of it seemed to help psychologically, and not just with me, but with the entire operating room team.

"I mean you didn't joke about the person on the operating table, but you would start to tell jokes about whatever popped into your mind, and at the worst possible time. Anyone on the outside listening in on those interactions between the surgical team would have thought us crude and callous. We were neither, but this was the only way we had to deal with the stress of the moment without breaking out in tears at the sheer amount of human devastation we were dealing with over there.

Years later, Hollywood would turn their scriptwriters loose on MASH units in the Korean War as subject matter for film projects. The show, appropriately enough, was called *M*A*S*H*, and it was a huge hit that began with a movie and evolved into one of the most popular TV shows in history.

The show revolved around Members of the 4077th Mobile Army Surgical Hospital unit caring for the injured. Key to the show's success was the operating room humor the doctors used to escape from the horror and depression of the situation.

Although MASH units were first introduced in the Korean War, it was Dick Virgilio and members of his Vietnam unit who consulted with the writers to make the movie and TV show *M*A*S*H* such a success and so morbidly funny. It was a brilliant example of art imitating life.

"No, of course that's not easy to deal with, but you do it and keep doing it because you know you're helping someone and making a difference in a difficult situation."

As Dick explained in retrospect, he never knew when his busy times were going to be. It's not as if he could predict Saturday nights were going to be busy because the knife and gun clubs would be out prowling. It could be any hour of the day or night.

"You would hear someone yelling over the loudspeakers,

'Incoming, incoming flights,' and then you would hear the whooping of the rotor blades. That's when we would all scramble into our positions.

* * *

"I had never seen that amount of blood before, never dealt with that amount of death. I had never been in a position to play God like that, you know, thumbs up or thumbs down, deciding who was going to get treatment—surgery. I worked with three really, really good surgeons over there, and a neurosurgeon who I wound up working with here at Balboa. It was a very good group of doctors.

"They took me under their wing because I had the least experience of anybody, but boy it didn't take me long to get experienced. I mean it's not like we were equipped for a teaching situation. You were thrown in and learned quickly, or else. It was like, see one, do one, teach someone else how to do one. You know? It was learning in the heat of battle—the deep end of the pool.

"Most everybody had a purpose—get along. And we were there for all kinds of reasons. There were people like me, who volunteered to be there. And there were people there because they got drafted and ordered to Vietnam. A lot of them were mad—angry at the fact that they had been drafted, ripped out of a very lucrative private practice, and sent to Vietnam.

"They had a hard time not showing animosity towards the system, towards the war. The politics of the war meant nothing to me. The only thing that was important to me was our guys were getting shot, and I was there to take care of them.

"I mean forget the question of whether or not we should be there, and forget taking notice of all the demonstrations going on back home. None of that meant anything to me. It was not even an issue. The only issue was that American soldiers were dying, and somebody had to be there to help take care of these guys.

"I had very mixed feelings about my own involvement to some

THE DICK VIRGILIO STORY

extent, only because I missed Bea, and I missed Maria so much. I'd cry at night thinking about them. We had no social media back then. You couldn't email anybody a picture, or text them with your phone. It was crazy. It was write a letter a day, every day, and then you'd wait to get mail, and that's what you would thrive on. You would live for mail call. Then you would go off in your little corner and have a moment.

* * *

"We had no real privacy over there. I lived in a Quonset hut on a cot, or a steel bed with a thin mattress on it, with a locker. There were people everywhere. There was a guy to my right, another guy to my left. There were guys at my feet.

"30 miles south of the heavy fighting."

"We didn't have the luxury of routines—like waking up, brushing our teeth, taking a shower, having breakfast or a cup of coffee, reading the morning newspaper, or even putting on a fresh set of clothes. I lived in my scrubs for days on end. If they got bloody, I put on a fresh set. I think I must have lived in scrubs my entire time there."

Dick was stationed in Da Nang, at what was known as China Beach. It was located 30 miles south of the heavy fighting. However, enemy mortar fire aimed at the adjacent helicopter base sometimes hit the hospital.

From July through Christmas it was hot, humid, and muggy. Two doctors, trying to cool off in the heat, were caught in an undertow while swimming at China Beach and drowned.

Towards springtime, the nights would get cooler, but then the Monsoons came and it rained for what seemed like forever. Everything turned to mud. Even the makeshift wooden walkways between the operating room and the intensive care unit would be deep in mud.

The intensity of their work created an extreme closeness in Dick's MASH unit. There were no female nurses, so there was never any

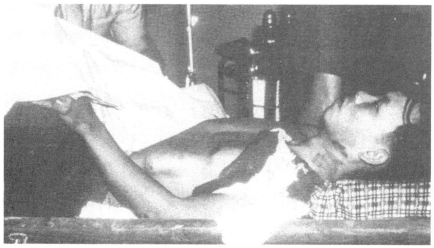

Patient as he appeared on admission, with mortar visible in chest wall.

conflict or distractions of that nature. Still, living in such close quarters created unique circumstances and ways of dealing with them.

"We had a few doctors who were prima donnas. You know, people who were drafted and didn't want to be there, people with temperament issues and inflated views of their importance. The corpsmen were great and extremely helpful. There wasn't a lot of fighting or jealousy among us. We were probably just too tired and had no time for that sort of thing. For the most part we were a nice little community."

Religion and church had not been a big part of Dick's life before Vietnam. That was about to change.

"I became pretty religious over there. How could you not under circumstances like that, where life and death were part of your every waking hour. I'd go to church services whenever I could. There was just so much devastation one man could take, so many things I'd never seen and hopefully will never see again. I met Father Joe Donald there. He was a great priest and friend who wound up back here at Balboa Hospital with me years later.

"I can remember operating on Vietnamese and opening their bellies and having all these worms crawl out, or worms burrowing their own hole out of a kid's gut. I came close to throwing up at times like that. But, other than being sick, I never actually threw up from what I saw or dealt with in my work."

Individual cases occasionally pop into Dick's mind. He remembers there were times when his team got irate soldiers who felt they deserved immediate care for some minor injury. Standard procedure would be to bring them into the operating theatre and show them what it meant to really be in need.

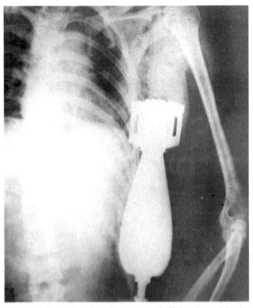

Chest X Ray showing the mortar shell implanted in the chest wall of a Vietnamese soldier.

Other times he might encounter a livid soldier screaming in his face because he felt Dick wasn't doing enough for his buddy. Same solution: Walk them behind the curtain so they see first-hand what the surgeons are dealing with day in and day out.

Another incident, in 1966, involved a South Vietnamese soldier who had the most freakish of incidents take place. While riding in an armored personnel carrier near Da Nang, an enemy mortar bounced off his steel helmet and penetrated the soft tissue between his shoulder and collarbone, then entered his body just below his left armpit.

The live round contained nearly two pounds of TNT. Had it gone off during surgery to remove it, the entire medical Quonset hut and all those inside would have been blown to smithereens.

The chief of surgery, Capt. Harry Dinsmore, evacuated the operating room except for ordnance specialists and volunteer surgeons assisting him in removing the live shell, which had also become twisted and wedged in with fragments of the soldier's shirt.

The operation was successful despite the firing pin of the mortar round being partially depressed upon entry. The soldier recovered and was back in the war within two months. Capt. Dinsmore was awarded the Navy Cross for his actions.

Dick was the doctor who admitted the patient and prepped him for surgery, took care of him in post op, and did the skin grafts to repair the wound. It's stories like that Dick won't ever forget. And he still wonders what happened to that soldier all these years later.

Still another case Dick will always remember is the young man who tried to commit suicide by shooting himself in the belly. The bullet severed his spinal cord, rendering him permanently paralyzed from the waist down.

"We worked on him for six or seven hours. During that period of time we had to triage two wounded marines who eventually died while we were operating on this guy who had tried to kill himself. As he was being carried out on the stretcher to be sent home, he pulled me in close and said, 'Look what you've done to me. You son of a bitch.' Then he spit at me. All I could think was, 'You piece of shit. People are dead because we worked to keep you alive.' "

Events like that changed the way Dick looked at life, and death, He no longer had sympathy for people who took their own lives. He knew it was wrong to feel that way about suicide, but the whole affair soured his way of thinking on that subject, and still does.

Likewise, Dick no longer pondered over cases where somebody had to make a decision to pull the plug on extreme cases. Later in his career he would always tell the new surgeons, as he encouraged them in their field, "There is only one thing worse than a bad decision, and that's no decision." That became Dick's mantra and remains so to this day.

"I never pretended to be God."

"Part of my responsibility in Vietnam was learning how not to prolong death. The problem with medicine today is nobody wants to say 'enough is enough.' Somebody's dead, but nobody is going to say it. The machine's blinking, the drips are going, everything is going, but the patient is gone.

"Well, I never pretended to be God. I never thought I was playing his role, but I certainly learned to realize when a person's time was up. To ignore that is to just prolong that guy's death and tie up more resources.

"Vietnam taught me to be more aggressive in life-and-death situations, but when I got home and saw the lack of decision going on in hospitals here, it was just insane. You'd have fifteen different doctors and nobody wanted to make the decision. It would infuriate me to hear a doctor ask the family if they wanted to take their loved one off the respirator.

"I would never ask a patient's family to make that decision. I won't put that burden on them, to have them carry that burden for the rest of their lives, or to condemn a patient to a lifetime of living on a respirator."

* * *

"I wasn't always so cut and dried about tough decisions. When I first got to Vietnam I was, 'Oh, yeah, let's do this, let's do that.' My ego didn't want to let a patient, any patient, get away from me.

"But I was thrown into an environment where you had to do things quickly, make decisions quickly, because other lives mattered, too. Other doctors over there may have had more experience operating than I did, but we all had to learn how to psychologically deal with what was going on in Vietnam and the sheer amount of death surrounding us.

"I had never seen so many severe burn wounds. A lot of our patients were burned when their troop carriers hit mines and exploded, spreading fuel and fire everywhere. As a general rule, you would never commit valuable resources on someone with eighty percent or more of their body burned, because they were going to die no matter what you did.

"Sadly, you would instruct the corpsman to find someplace quiet for them, make them as comfortable as possible, and put the patient on a morphine drip while a priest was summoned. When the patient died, I would come over and officially pronounce the death.

"We had a Catholic priest and Protestant chaplain on hand most of the time. They would administer last rites on the patients, and you could hear that low murmur of prayers in the background 24/7. When they weren't dealing with wounded and dying, they spent a lot of time psychoanalyzing the staff, making sure we were okay, checking our stress levels."

* * *

Over a typical 24-hour day the surgeons at China Beach would do ten to fifteen operations. Most of the operations performed were gut shots, chest wounds, and amputations. The long bowel resects were the worst. It took seemingly forever for surgeons to repair the damage caused by shrapnel shredding the human body. They would cut away certain segments and repair holes in others.

As the Marines operating north of Da Nang were getting the stuffing shot out of them, China Beach was their only hope of surviving a life-threatening wound.

"That's when they started doing what we called 'scooping and hauling.' In the Korean War, the war prior to Vietnam, they had these little aid station outposts where they would try to treat the bad casualties before moving them to a second tier facility. It didn't work.

"Those little first-aid stations couldn't carry enough medical supplies or equipment to make a difference, and men were dying. So in Vietnam they started scooping and hauling, bringing them back by way of helicopters to a definitive care hospital, like ours in Da Nang. Time is always the difference between life and death.

"We were fortunate at our hospital to have everything we needed, plus some. We couldn't put somebody on a cardiopulmonary bypass machine, or an artificial lung, but as far as equipment went, blood and fluid machines, suture material, and instruments, we were in good shape.

"The majority of surgeries we encountered were injuries from landmines, blast wounds, and bullet wounds. Like I said, we did an awful lot of bowel resections and liver injuries, as well as vascular injuries to the extremities that resulted in a vast number of amputations.

"Since we only had two orthopedic surgeons on staff, if you had a patient with a severe extremity injury, and the orthopedic surgeons were tied up, you just finished what the explosive started, concluding the amputation, dressing up the wound as best you could, and that was the end of it.

"We had no ophthalmologist, so when encountering any kind of bad eye injury we had no choice but to enucleate the eye—take it out. I would also assist the neurosurgeon a lot of the time because he had no one to help him. So I ended up doing a lot of head wound surgeries, chest wounds, and amputations, and just a general run of the gauntlet.

"In a twenty-four-hour period, you might find yourself operating non-stop. Your adrenaline kicks in and you think, 'Shit, I'll never be able to stay awake for this one,' and then all of a sudden you're just doing it, and the adrenaline keeps you pumping. That, and we drank a lot of coffee. If you were lucky, you could lie down on a cot or on the floor for an hour while the room was being cleaned up for the next surgery.

"For thirteen months in Vietnam I got to experience things I couldn't have experienced anywhere else. Professionally speaking, it was probably the best year of my life, regardless of the fact that I was away from my family."

Post-traumatic stress disorder has become commonplace in our vernacular when discussing our troops coming home. It wasn't officially recognized as a mental health condition until 1980, although symptoms have been documented under different names for hundreds of years. Dick, fortunately, was one of the lucky ones.

"Coming home, I just always felt that if you were weak when you came back, you were weak when you went, that if you needed help when you came back, you probably needed help when you left the States. Sure, the transition was hard, and I was maybe more moody at first, but I didn't dwell on it. I didn't make it a disability for myself, and time ended up being the best healer.

"What I saw was gruesome. It was terrible. But I'm not going to have nightmares about it. I'm strong in, strong out. That's the way I always felt about it—strong in, strong out. Coming home, I never had a problem with dreaming about my days in Vietnam, but for years to follow, I'd freak out at the sound of helicopter blades."

Dick and Hal Dinsmor, his boss and the surgeon who removed the mortar, along with patient preparing to be discharged back to duty.

ELEVEN

The Lighter Side of Vietnam

The tradition of playing music during medical procedures dates back to the ancient Greeks. In the early 1900s a surgeon placed a phonograph in the operating room to calm and distract his patients.

In Korea and Vietnam, operating room music served to keep the surgeons alert and awake—to keep that all-valuable adrenaline coursing through their bodies and help them to work on the edge when their bodies were ready to collapse from exhaustion. It was never more prevalent than in the operating rooms of China Beach.

In the 1960s, vinyl records were being challenged by four-track tape players. By 1965, the more durable eight-track tape players hit the market and were the rage, as they would play both sides of an album and then repeat automatically—a hands-free operation taking up less space.

But, for Dick and his China Beach comrades, that would come later. During his tenure in Vietnam, Armed Forces Radio was their only source of music and news. Servicemen served as disc jockeys, programming one-hour shows to entertain the troops, as highlighted in the movie, *Good Morning, Vietnam.*

Popular songs included "Wooly Bully" by Sam the Sham and the Pharaohs, "Satisfaction" by the Rolling Stones, and Barry McGuire's "Eve of Destruction." Armed Forces Radio famously played the song

"White Christmas" as a signal for Americans that the final evacuation of Saigon had begun in April 1975.

"Music was a major part of the climate in our operating rooms," Dick recalled. "The rooms were pretty close together. Two Quonset huts sat next to each other, not quite separate rooms. The corpsmen pretty much managed the music for us, but we could hear the other operating suite's music, and they could hear ours. Consequently, there was a lot of bitching and fighting about what song to play or whose turn it was to change the music, or even how loud it played."

Alcohol played an important role in Hollywood's *M*A*S*H*, but not so for the doctors and corpsmen in Vietnam.

"That wasn't the case with us. Every so often we might get scheduled for twelve hours of down time, unless there was an absolute catastrophe unfolding. At times like that, in theory, you could kick back and have a few drinks, but you could never drink so much that you couldn't leap into action in case of an emergency. It wasn't like the TV show, where doctors kept booze hidden in their lockers.

"At times like that, which were rare, my drink was scotch on the rocks, with a splash of water. We had a little officer's club over there. It was a small Quonset hut where they had a pool table and some games. It had a little library there where you could read and check out books, and you might watch a movie. We showed movies on Beta [videotape], which was the latest thing back then.

"Clearly you didn't have a Sunday afternoon free for golf or other recreational things, but at times we would head down to the beach and swim or just lie around on the sand."

* * *

Life to a MASH surgeon was generally spent in intense working situations, with the grim reaper hovering over every patient, waiting to collect his next victim. One episode that Dick will never forget took place outside the typical drama of the landmines and chest wounds of the operating theatre. It involved working on a Vietnamese prisoner

This 1966 photo captures Dick standing outside the surgical ward at the Naval Hospital in Danang, Vietnam.

of war—a member of the Vietcong.

"I had a close friend, Will Lathum, who was a surgeon like me, but had been a plastic surgeon in civilian life. He was always looking for people he could help on his own time. We would go to the orphanage and find kids with cleft lips, and he would take them down to the hospital, borrow a little local anesthesia and fix the kid's lip.

"One time he decided to help a North Vietnamese prisoner who came in with a belly wound. We operated and fixed his belly, but his face was a mess. His nose was way off to the side from what appeared to be old injuries from the French-Vietnam conflict years earlier (1946-1954). It drove Will crazy looking at this guy, so he decided to do something about it.

"The problem was that Will's time was up. He was going home the next morning. So he comes and gets me about ten p.m. and tells me he can't leave and go home, knowing he might have been able to help that POW.

"Well, shit. I knew I had to help him, even though this soldier's job had been to kill Americans, and he probably was good at it. So we grabbed a corpsman and spent three hours putting this guy's face back together. Will wrapped him all up so just his eyes and mouth were visible. He told me to unwrap it in ten days.

"We bring him back to the heavily guarded holding area for POWs in the middle of the night, and, judging from all the bandages on his face, they're all looking at us like we've just tortured this poor bastard.

"Will's last words to me were, 'Dick, do me one more favor please. Take a photo of his face when the bandages come off and send it to me.' So, sure as hell, ten days later I remove the bandages. All the other POWs were watching my every move. As the bandages fell away he looked like a new person. He still had sutures and residuals from the operation, but his nose was where it was supposed to be, and you could hear the other prisoners gasping at what they saw.

"I held up a mirror, and I'll never forget that moment. He looked in that mirror and started to cry. He uttered something very emotional in Vietnamese. While I couldn't tell what he was saying, I can imagine. This soldier had a face that was difficult to look upon for the prior decade, and now he didn't.

"Shortly thereafter all the prisoners were loaded on a big truck and moved elsewhere, so I don't know what happened to that fellow. But I took the photo and sent it to Will. I'm sure that was a bright moment from an otherwise bloody and messy war for him. I know it was for me."

* * *

This was obviously a time before cell phones, Facetime, and satellite communications. In many parts of the world, simple telephone connections to the outside world were difficult to impossible. Vietnam was one of those places.

When our American forces in Vietnam wanted to contact someone at home, they worked through a HAM radio operator, who would relay the signal to another operator, and eventually (hopefully) contact their loved ones.

"It was November. I had been there a few months and decided I'd try to call home and talk to Bea. You had to go into this big room and pick a number, you know, just like you were at the grocery store meat counter, and they would call you up when it was your turn.

"They place the call, and then you sit and wait for the connection to come through. There was another HAM operator in Midway who could patch through calls for the guys to their families, and once or twice a week our hospital would be designated to place a call. It would have been Sunday morning where Bea was when I tried to call.

"The place was always packed and both sides of the conversation were blasted into the room by overhead speakers, so there was no privacy whatsoever.

"My mother-in-law, who was down visiting with Bea and Maria, answered the call. She couldn't understand why I was in Vietnam and her daughter and granddaughter were in Silver Spring, Maryland. I mean, that totally went beyond her ability to reason. She's the one, if you'll remember, who didn't want me to marry her daughter because I was going to be a doctor.

"Well, as is typical on such calls, there is a lot of static, and you try to speak over it, but often you can't hear what's being said. It's a nightmare. And you're only allowed ten minutes of talk, and half of that is spent saying after each sentence, 'Over,' or 'Can you repeat that? Over.'

"For chrissake, you knocked up her daughter!"

"Then I hear her scream, 'Dick, you've got to get home right away. You've got to get home now.' Well, by that point, everyone in the room with me is rolling on the floor laughing, so I said out loud, 'Oh, Christ, what's happened?' She said Bea was at church and asked where I was. 'Vietnam, mother.' And she said, 'Where's that?' More laughter from the peanut gallery.

"She keeps talking, but because of the static, I can't hear a word she's saying. Finally I yell, 'Mother, I can't hear a word you're saying . . . over.'

"About that time the HAM operator in Midway breaks in and says, 'For chrissake, you knocked up her daughter! What the hell else do you need to know pal?'

"Well, as you can imagine, the room full of guys I'm with erupts into laughter again. They're laughing their off. 'Yeah right, Doc, you knocked up the poor lady's daughter and then ran off to Vietnam. No wonder you volunteered. Ha ha ha ha.' The guys were ruthless, and man was that embarrassing.

"So that's how I found out that Bea was pregnant with Angela, our second child, who would be three months old by the time I got home."

* * *

Dick had a couple of other bright spots during his 13 months of hell at China Beach.

"Angela was born in April, so, in the early part of March, six or eight weeks before she was born, I had a chance to go on R&R (rest and recuperation).

"They used to send us for four days to either Thailand, Hong Kong, or Japan on those rare occasions we weren't too busy. They would take you out of the hospital, put you in civilian clothes because they didn't want the Japanese to know how many military were in their city, then put you on an airplane.

"So, I told Bea in a letter, which was virtually the only sure way to communicate, that I was going to be on four days of R&R. I knew by then she was pretty far along in her pregnancy, but told her to check with her doctor and maybe she could join me in Tokyo.

"Her doctor advised her against it, but she was determined, and in the end her doctor granted her permission to fly. I had a lady in Da Nang arrange my flights and a hotel, and I mailed all that information to Bea.

"Bea was going to fly in the night before. When I got to the hotel, they said there was no one by her name there. 'Oh, Christ,' I thought. Here I am in the middle of Tokyo by myself, looking forward to seeing my wife that I hadn't seen in eight months, who is practically due with the baby, and I don't know where the hell she is.

"Then the front desk manager told me she had checked out because she didn't like the room.

"I'm almost in tears."

"Well, you've got to understand Bea. I've never been in a hotel with her where we've ever stayed in the same room that we checked in to. She always wants this view or that view, or something isn't right about this hotel.

"The front desk manager said, she went to the Hilton Hotel. So I got in the damned cab and went to the Hilton Hotel.

"I said I was looking for Mrs. Virgilio, and the guy at the desk says there is no one here by that name. By this time I'm totally exhausted from work and the long flight, I'm in a foreign city with millions of people, and I'm almost in tears. So I ask for a small room for myself to rest and regroup before I start to search for her again. While I'm filling out the ledger, he screams, 'Ohhhhhh, Virgilio. I thought you said Birgilio. Your wife is in room four-oh-six.'

"When we finally connected, we laughed so hard you wouldn't believe it. I thought I was going to have a heart attack. I got to see my wife and hold her, and hold her belly with my child still in the womb. We didn't know whether it would be a boy or a girl, but if it were a girl we wanted to name her Angela.

"We had a great time. Bea flew home at the end of four days, and three weeks later she had the baby. The navy somehow found a way to get me a photo of the newborn immediately. I don't know how they did it, but when they brought it to me in the Quonset hut, I just cried and cried. I swore right then and there that I would never miss the birth of another of my children, that I would never not be there for Bea again."

* * *

Coming home, Dick had time to reflect on the past year in great detail.

"That thirteen months went pretty fast. I certainly learned a lot about my own psychological stamina, and my physical stamina. I learned a lot about medicine—about surgery. I came home a much better doctor, and I think a much better person. I began to realize over there how valuable life was, and how lucky I was. I think it was the best professional year of my career, and I wouldn't have traded that experience for anything.

"I did more good for people in that one year than I did in the next 30 years. I learned about my ability to deal with adversity and separation from my family. As a result, I had a lot more respect for Bea than I ever had before, for what she went through, and what she did while I was gone, and how she kept those two girls. I mean, she had both girls for three months before I got home and, yeah, it was a pivotal year in my career and my life."

For Dick, there was no particular transition from Vietnam to the States and civilian life. Typical of the time, soldiers and doctors alike returned carrying a lot of stress and a lot of memories.

"I think the hardest thing about coming back was you couldn't really describe or relate your experience to anybody that hadn't been there.

"I mean, you couldn't go to a dinner party and have a conversation about putting limbs back together, about prolonging death, about watching people die, and triaging people who are probably just not gonna make it. There was no one to ventilate to, and, in hindsight, that was probably not healthy for me.

"I came back, but the only time I could talk about Vietnam was if I met somebody else who had been a surgeon there, and we could talk about those experiences. That, however, was rare.

"It was certainly harder for me to reenter this society than it was to be plopped down in Da Nang. Because once I got there, it was like, here's a scrub suit and a pair of gloves, go to work.

"Here I had time to think. I probably should have sought out some therapy, but I didn't. Today they call it post-traumatic stress disorder, or syndrome. We knew so little about that in those days. Fortunately for me, I was luckier than most."

* * *

One irony of civilian life with roots in Vietnam occurred years later when Dick helped his daughter Christina sail her boat across the Atlantic Ocean. They were sailing from St. Maarten in the Caribbean to San Remo in Italy, and there was a new chef on board, a Vietnamese fellow about 35 or 40 years old.

"I couldn't believe how well this fellow got around on the boat. He had one leg, amputated above the knee, and, even though he wore the prosthesis with an artificial knee on it, he went up and down the ladder as well or better than any of the rest of us with two good legs.

"I got on the boat in St. Maarten. They introduced me to him, and we started talking. I asked him how he lost his leg, and he said it was a land mine in Vietnam. He said he was an orphan in Da Nang when his parents got killed in an explosion. His leg had been severely injured in the explosion, and doctors had to remove it.

"In those days, several American families adopted injured Vietnamese kids and brought them to the States for a formal education and a better life. As it happened, this was the lucky kid who was adopted by a wealthy family in Philadelphia.

"He ends up getting fitted with a prosthesis, learns English, receives a formal education, and attends culinary school. Now he's a first-class chef and speaks perfect English. So I asked him how old he was when he lost his leg.

"After some figuring, it became evident to me that he lost his leg during my tenure in Vietnam. I did ninety percent of the amputations on Vietnamese kids back then, and it turns out I did the amputation of this kid's leg, nearly 20 years earlier."

TWELVE

Discovering the World of Boating

After Vietnam, Dick returned to an entirely new world. It was 1967 and by then he had two children, one of whom didn't recognize him, and the other he had yet to meet. He and Bea had to make some tough decisions about their future—what they would do, and where.

"I remember vividly the trip home because I came back on a medical evacuation flight that flew virtually nonstop from Da Nang to Andrews Air Force Base. My work in Vietnam was far from over. I had a bunch of sick patients on the plane with me.

"After two months in Vietnam, I had kept my head shaved because it was so damned hot, and it was just easier to care for. A friend of mine, Vic, was a neurosurgeon, and he shaved all of his patients' heads before surgeries. One day I told him I couldn't stand it any longer, so he shaved my head, too.

"Well, Bea saw that and flipped out. She told me I had the ugliest head in the world, and that I had better get a wig, because my baldhead just wasn't going to work for her. "My hair eventually grew back.

While I was away, my second daughter, Angela, was born. So I came home to a one-year old and a three-month old.

"I had never seen Angela, and hadn't seen Maria for thirteen months. So it was quite a reintroduction for me, and to a completely different kind of life and pace.

"I mean, here I am, in a home, with two little kids in my lap. I had been living in a Quonset hut with a bunch of guys and working my rear end off for more than a year. All of a sudden I'm walking into a house, which I had only lived in for six months before I went to Vietnam, and two little babies live there.

"The worst part was that Maria, my oldest, wouldn't have anything to do with me. She hadn't been around anybody but Bea for a year. She was three months old when I left her and, well, she didn't remember me, and that hurt. That really hurt. When I first got home, she would cry anytime I'd come near her, and wanted nothing to do with me.

"So I had to back off and just realize that with time it would change. I began to focus my attention on this blonde-haired, blue-eyed baby, Angela.

"It seems funny now, but I had no idea where the heck Angela came from. As far as I knew, when I left the States Bea wasn't even pregnant. Well, she was, but I didn't know it.

"One day I'm sitting in our bay window having coffee and breakfast, and all of a sudden the doorbell rings. I open the door, and here's the mailman, with blonde hair and blue eyes. Now I'm thinking, 'Self? He looks an awful lot like your daughter.'

"So I finally get up the nerve to ask Bea why the postman comes in the house, and why he doesn't just drop mail in the mailbox like normal mailmen.

"She laughed and said he liked children, and always came in to see the kids. Of course, it didn't take me long to realize that Angela was every bit of me."

As Dick struggled to settle into home life and being a father, secretly he dealt with symptoms of what was known as "shell shock" in World War II—more familiarly known since 1980 as Post-Traumatic Stress Disorder (PTSD).

Essentially, PTSD is a mental health condition that is triggered by a stressful or terrifying event or series of events. It expresses itself in many ways that can include flashbacks, nightmares, depression, severe anxiety, and even suicidal tendencies.

"I certainly never thought about my situation as post-traumatic stress at the time, but I did know that what I had been through I couldn't relate to just anyone at a cocktail party or on the street. You just couldn't talk about guys with their limbs blown off and burned to a crisp, or making life-and-death decisions to triage them or put them aside to die.

"Strong in, strong out."

"On the rare occasion I ran into another doctor who had been through similar experiences, we could talk freely, and yet there was no special program to transition doctors from war to civilian life—to deal with that sort of baggage. And it wasn't just me. All of us had to return and deal with it in our own way."

Fortunately for Dick, the effects of PTSD were minor. His motto was, "Strong in, strong out." He believed the individuals who went into that situation strong, came out of it strong. That was the way he dealt with his entire life—strong in, strong out.

"Yeah, you can't let it keep you awake at night worrying about it. You've got to do your best to put it behind you, to deal with it. In my case, we couldn't save everybody. We saved some, some died. But we had to keep moving forward with our own lives.

"You had to be tolerant with those around you, because they had no idea, and couldn't imagine what you had been through. It just took awhile. I couldn't even talk to Bea about it. But the only severe reaction I can recall is when I would hear a helicopter overhead. I would really freak out when that happened, for obvious reasons.

"Eventually I would look for other doctors who had been there, and we would go out and have a beer and bullshit about it all. That became an important part of my life after Vietnam. I think I was one of the fortunate ones. I never felt incapacitated by my experiences—never looked at it like a syndrome. It was just there, and I dealt with it the best I could—strong in, strong out."

* * *

Dick had a month of leave after Vietnam, hardly enough time to cope with all the changes in his life, but plenty of time for him to get his feet back on the ground and begin to crave going back to work. He truly loved the work he did. Although his young family was his life, he took immense pleasure in helping the sick and injured.

Two years later, in 1969, his third child, Christianna, was born. Dick was in the operating room with a patient and missed her birth, just as he had missed Maria's birth because of his work. He had missed Angela's birth because he was in Vietnam.

"Suddenly, I had three little girls, and even though I had missed their actual deliveries, the time I did spend at home with Bea and the children was quality time and I loved it.

"After Christianna's birth, I got reassigned to take over the critical care and trauma unit at Balboa Hospital in San Diego. So, with a two-year-old, four-year-old, and five-year-old, we headed west and said our good-byes to Bethesda, Maryland.

"It was a challenge for us. Bea wasn't overly thrilled. She was born and raised on the East Coast. Her family was all on the East Coast. Her sister had lived across the street from us, and suddenly her support network was gone.

"We loaded up the old Chrysler station wagon and headed to a place Bea and the children had never seen before, San Diego. It was about this time I began to alter my sleeping habits. I would take over the wheel about 9 p.m. and drive for twelve hours. That way I didn't have to drive and listen to the three kids all day long.

"In the morning, I'd check us into a hotel with a swimming pool, and Bea and the kids would play around all day while I took a nap.

"In San Diego, we found a beautiful home in Bonita and bought it. What we failed to realize was how much higher the cost of living was on the West Coast. This was 1971, and I couldn't make it on the $33,000 a year I was making in the navy, so I took on two moonlighting jobs at hospitals in South Bay.

"I was basically working three jobs. I was full-time at Balboa, and I'd work nights in the emergency room (ER) at Bay General Hospital or Chula Vista Community Hospital to make extra money. In what little time I could squeeze in, I did insurance physicals at patients' homes."

Shortly after moving to Bonita, the Virgilios had a fourth child, a boy they named Joseph.

"In those days we didn't know if the baby was going to be a boy or a girl. Just as Bea goes into labor, I get an emergency call that a patient has a ruptured aneurism, so I got up to leave Bea and go back to work.

"Meanwhile, Bea's screaming at me that this will be my last opportunity to see one of my children being born, as we had agreed four was enough, and that she would have her tubes tied.

"Bob Brown was the obstetrician, and I begged him to do something, to give Bea some Pitocin to hurry the baby along, so I could see it come out before I had to prepare for surgery.

"Suddenly, there he was. I saw little Joe come out. I saw his little tweaker down there, and knew I had a son. That was a very, very special moment for me. We nicknamed him "Son Boy."

"I couldn't stay long because I had to get to my surgery. Bob Brown said he would take care of the tubal ligation. That was fine with me. I had four kids and three jobs, and figured our family was complete.

* * *

"My son was born in 1972, a year after we got to San Diego. Bea had her tubes tied, and we were going about our business. I was still working three jobs, with very little time to be home, but trying to give my kids as much attention as I could.

"Fortunately for me, Bea took care of all the home stuff. The kids started school. We had an acre there in Bonita, with a corral up at the top, so we got a horse.

"While we were far from your typical American family, our life was pretty cool. It was a nice feeling to leave the hospital and go back there at the end of the day."

The Virgilio home was located in a beautiful part of South San Diego Bay. In those days it was wide-open space, grassy fields, and large shade trees. Their new home was located just above the old Bonita Store. In addition to a horse and pony, they had a swimming pool.

It was close to the city, yet as country as anyone could ask for. It was a safe place to raise a family, and the children had lots of places to ride horseback. The 805 Freeway had yet to be built. Southwestern Junior College had just opened, but Otay Lakes and the vast surrounding areas were virtually undeveloped—wide-open land.

Then, in early 1974, a little more than a year after Joe was born, Bea was not feeling well, and not looking well.

"She's in pain and is throwing up, and, Jesus, we didn't know what was the matter," Dick said. "She thought she had cancer.

"As it turns out, she was pregnant with our fifth child, Gina. Keep in mind, this is after my buddy tied her tubes. I couldn't believe it. We had four children, I was working exhausting hours, and I just didn't know how on earth we were going to handle another child. But we managed."

* * *

In the summer of 1974, four years before Dick's retirement from the Navy, the Virgilio family was growing in multiple directions. Bea was scheduled to give birth to her fifth child, and Dick was still working three jobs to make ends meet.

A summer tradition they became fond of was to join other doctors and their families in taking the Catalina Express from Newport Beach to Catalina Island, where they would rent a small cottage.

Dick was playing in the pool with his son, Joe, one afternoon. A favorite thing to do was to hold Joe in his arms and jump off the diving board.

"I had Joe in my arms, jumping off the diving board, and when I hit the water I got this god-awful pain in my chest. At first I thought it was because I reached up to grab the board or something. But it was much worse.

"For several months I had noticed a decrease in my stamina, and some vague chest discomfort, but nothing like I experienced that day. We finished our trip, but it turned out to be the first real cardiac episode I can recall.

"I remember being really tired at the time, so I didn't say anything. But when we got back to San Diego, and summer progressed, my symptoms worsened. I went to see my friend, who was a cardiologist, and told him I thought something was the matter with my chest.

"He said I couldn't possibly have anything wrong because I was just thirty-six years old. I insisted that something was very wrong in my chest. He countered with, 'Well, how are things going at home? I know Bea's pregnant with your fifth child, and it must be very stressful for you. And you're working an awful lot.'

"I told him again that I just didn't feel good, that there was a problem, so he pulled out his stethoscope, which was about as ineffective as you could get, examination-wise. 'You're fine,' he said, 'your blood pressure is good, your lungs sound good, and your heart sounds good.'

"I went back to work the next day, but during the course of my rounds I would feel this pressure in my chest. Still, I couldn't convince anybody I had a problem and, here I am, a doctor, surrounded by other doctors, and unable to convince them that my symptoms were real."

* * *

Dick quickly lost himself in work, but he couldn't get Catalina off his mind. Despite the chest pains, he and the family had had a really good time there.

Catalina has long been a summer haven for vacationing boaters. Early on, the island belonged to Mexico. It was sporadically used for smuggling, sea otter hunting, and gold prospecting, before being developed as a tourist destination by chewing gum magnate William Wrigley, Jr., in the Roaring Twenties.

It did not go unnoticed by Dick that, while vacationing in Catalina, the people having the most fun were those on their boats. It appealed to him in a big way.

After their return to San Diego, Dick made the drive to Coronado to visit a friend at Fiddler's Cove—a yacht club for retired military personnel on the Silver Strand.

At Fiddler's, the tallest boat there was an old Luders yawl, one of the few surviving, 44-foot yawls designed for use as the U.S. Naval Academy's sail training fleet in the 1930s. Dick's friend had access to it and invited him and his family for a sail one afternoon.

"It was such a big and beautiful sailboat, but I had never sailed in my life. Once we got underway, it was so soothing, so quiet, and I thought it was just the neatest thing ever. We sailed up into Glorietta Bay to the Coronado Yacht Club, where they were celebrating their Opening Day.

"As soon as we got back, I started thinking about buying a boat. Now, you have to realize this about me, when I get something in my mind that I want to do, I do it. So I told Bea we were going to go boat hunting.

"She tried to talk me out of it with the usual argument: 'You're working three jobs.' And I told her I would work four jobs if I had to, just to get us a boat. My argument was that we, as a family, didn't do anything together. And I made my plea that when I come home exhausted, how nice it would be to go for a relaxing sail in the evenings.

"Bea quickly pointed out that I didn't even know anyone who had a boat. But, how difficult could it be, I thought. It's not brain surgery. Of course, I found out later that it was more difficult than brain surgery, but we started visiting Shelter Island and looking at boats right away.

"I didn't know port from starboard."

"One day we looked at a 30-foot Coronado for sale at Fraser's Yacht Sales. A guy named Hugo Shriner owned it. I didn't know it at the time, but he was a very famous Olympic sailor. He and his wife had separated, and he was living on the boat.

"I can't remember what I paid for it, and it didn't matter at the time. I went to the bank, borrowed the money, and bought this crazy boat. It came with a slip at Fraser's, so I was able to keep it there.

"Then it suddenly dawned on me that I didn't know how to sail, so I quickly negotiated into the price of the sailboat that Hugo would have to give me five sailing lessons. He agreed.

"The weekend came around, and Hugo took pregnant Bea and me, and all four kids, up and down the bay. I gotta say, I didn't know port from starboard. I didn't know what a tack was, a jibe, or anything. The worst part was, I couldn't get that little boat into the slip, either. I kept banging into everyone else at Fraser's, and it was just hysterical.

"But the Virgilio family had a boat, and that was all that mattered to me. I would get better at sailing, and the only way I knew that is because clearly I couldn't get any worse."

Dick was still under Hugo's guidance at sea and had yet to sail his own boat. The family didn't quite share his joy for sailing, not just yet. Nevertheless, he had his boat, and it made him very happy.

Fast-forward a month. In August, chest pains once again brought Dick to his knees as he was making patient rounds in the ICU. His face grew ashen, and the cardiologist making the rounds with him quickly arranged for Dick to check into the cardiac unit. There, they ran the series of tests. Despite the debilitating pain Dick felt, every test result came back absolutely normal.

"Suddenly, my life had changed. I found myself in this coronary care unit, proud owner of a new boat that nobody wanted. The kids didn't want it. Bea didn't want it. Our fifth child is just weeks away, and my friend the cardiologist is telling me there is nothing the matter with my heart.

"I said, 'Vic, there is something going on in my chest.' And then he would launch again into, 'Well, how are things going at home. We know that Bea's having this child,' and then he suggested that we probably didn't want the child, and that the pressure of that was adding to the stress in my life—that it was all in my head, hinting that I might need psychiatric help.

"Well, that really pissed me off. I told him in no uncertain terms that we definitely wanted this child, and that I wasn't going to see a shrink.

"Finally, I called another friend, a heart surgeon, and told him that, while I knew he thought me a little crazy, that I would gladly see a psychiatrist if his team would do an angiogram on me and show me my arteries. If my arteries showed wide open and clear, I told him I'd gladly see the shrink."

Dick told the surgical team that he wasn't going to get out of that bed until they did this, and he convinced the cardiologist to do the procedure. Fortunately, Dick's friend lobbied his cause, and the cardiology team agreed.

Dick's procedure was scheduled ten days before the birth of their fifth child.

In hindsight, the medical team's apprehension stemmed from an incident that took place earlier that year during a cardiac cauterization.

Angiograms were very new at that time, just as heart surgery in general was in its infancy. There was a certain risk factor with angiograms, not to mention the discomfort. No one wanted to box a 36-year-old doctor (send him to the grave) because of an unnecessary test such as that.

"I told them they would do well to remember why Willie Sutton robbed banks—because that's where the money was. They finally relented and agreed to perform a cauterization (where I told them they would find the money)."

Sutton's Law is probably more familiar to doctors than the average person. It suggests that, when diagnosing, you should first consider the obvious—conduct those tests that could confirm or rule out the most likely diagnosis.

Medical schools teach Sutton's Law to impress upon students to order tests in that sequence most likely to result in a quick diagnosis or treatment, while minimizing unnecessary costs or risks.

To better illustrate the risk factor of such a test in 1974, doctors would insert a catheter in an artery—which violated a normal artery—then inject dye into the patient's aorta. Patients undergoing the angiogram had developed serious reactions to this invasion to their system. The procedure had been known to cause arrhythmia, and even a heart attack, depending on the patient's condition.

"A priest came in and gave me last rites."

"They wheeled me downstairs. A priest came in and gave me last rites. Bea, of course, just freaked out at this. I looked down at the doctor at the foot of my bed. Standing next to him is Bea, with this big belly, pregnant with our fifth child. All four of my little rug rats are sitting there.

"I remember clearly saying goodbye to Bea, and saying goodbye to my four children as I was being wheeled down for the procedure. I couldn't help but think this fifth child might have been God's way of replacing me in the family.

"I had a life-changing moment then and there. Up to that point, I had grown to feel that I was a hot-shit surgeon—someone pretty damn special, if not irreplaceable.

"Call it the environment, the amount of patients I had to deal with, the quick rise from medical school to battlefield surgeon to trauma specialist, or whatever you want. But at that moment, as I helplessly looked at my family and the sadness in their faces, I realized that my priorities had become confused over the years.

"It hit me like a rock in the head that the only thing that made me unique was the fact that there was nobody who could be the husband to Bea and the father to my children but me.

"I said, 'Self? If you are lucky enough to survive this operation, you better get your shit together and put family first and profession second."

The catheterization process began. As if the surgery wasn't painful enough for him to deal with—going against the popular tide of thought from his contemporaries in the medical field—Dick remembers lying there awake in the Cath Lab, listening to his friends talk about his decision to undergo this risky surgery as opposed to sitting down on a psychiatrist's couch.

Suddenly one of them exclaimed, "Oh, shit! Can you believe this? He's got a widow-producing lesion. Let's get him to the operating room, NOW!"

The widow-maker lesion involves the left anterior descending artery about to occlude (close up). If that happens, you die. Oftentimes it happens to people on the street, and they just fall over dead. Bang. And no one ever knew they had a heart disorder.

The surgery was successful. The very talented surgical team, made up of Dick's friends and professional peers, fixed the artery and performed a double heart bypass. As Dick was recovering and about to be released and sent home, Bea went into labor and had their fifth child.

"This was God's way of giving me a second chance. I had such a bad taste in my mouth from my own father, and the way he treated our family, and I wanted so desperately to be a good father. But, apparently, I wasn't starting out very good. I wasn't paying attention as I should have."

"That's God punishing you for marrying a doctor."

On that date, in August 1974, Dick Virgilio underwent a complete change in his life. At age 36, in the prime of life, and with a new baby due in just a week's time, Dick had the first of what would be multiple heart operations. This, indeed, became the event that would change his approach to life forever, and define how he lived the remainder of his life.

A week after Dick's successful surgery, Bea gave birth to another beautiful girl. They named her Gina Rose and knew that this little girl was a gift from the Lord. No one appreciated that fact more than Dick.

"Bea's mother, of course, being the staunch Catholic she was, got so mad at Bea for getting her tubes tied. She said, 'That's God punishing you for marrying a doctor and for getting your tubes tied.' I tell you, my mother-in-law was a piece of work.

"When I returned to work at Balboa Hospital, we had a huge residency program where I was very involved in teaching. Every one of those residents came up and wished me well. They all chipped in and bought me this enormous wooden ship's helm, because they knew I had this stupid boat. So I had to come to grips with the boat. I figured I had better start using it."

* * *

Getting the entire family to go sailing seemed a good idea at first. After a long, slow recovery, Dick dragged all his kids, and Bea, complete with bassinet and baby, on to their 30-foot boat.

After about three times out, it became clear to him (and to Bea) that this boat was not nearly big enough for seven people. So he went looking once again. He upgraded to a Columbia 36.

"San Diego Yacht Club was accepting military members at that time, so I joined. Of course, I still knew nothing about sailing my boat, and didn't know a single soul in the boating world, or at San Diego Yacht Club. But it was a start."

Dick made friends quickly and began to pour his Type-A personality into this new world of sailing. He quickly figured out the difference between bow and stern, port and starboard.

They practiced man-overboard drills and he learned to sail to

The Virgilios' second boat, Bea Hive, *in 1975.*

weather and to run downwind with the best of them. His confidence grew exponentially with each hour spent on the water.

It was still 1974 and Dick had a new life in more ways than one. In a very short time, he had gone from a day sail at Fiddler's to being a boat owner, to being a member in good standing at the prestigious San Diego Yacht Club.

He continued to practice military medicine and work on developing a much-needed trauma recovery system that would soon take on a life of its own throughout the county. But at that time, his priority was family, and his passion was sailing. Lingering close to the surface of everything he did, however, was the reality that his heart was defective, and the knowledge that he had almost died, and could again.

"After the surgery I was scared. I was really scared, because they told me that my chances of living to fifty weren't very good. I was given a second lease on life, and by God I wasn't going to squander it.

"I broke stereotype wherever I went."

"Not only did I change in how I spent time with my family, and how I poured myself into this new pastime of sailing, I became a better doctor. I began to break stereotype wherever I went. My own medical challenges had, in fact, changed my entire approach to patients.

"Suddenly, we all realized you absolutely could have heart disease under fifty years of age. It was a medical revelation of sorts in our world. Rapidly, we began to see more and more young people getting angiograms and experiencing heart disease, then living full lives, if, they were lucky enough to get diagnosed and treated.

"The same with cancer. If a twenty-four-year-old girl came in with a lump in her breast, you could no longer assume it wasn't cancer because she was only twenty-four. Now we know that twenty-four -year-old girls can have cancer.

"Here I was, a doctor with ten-years of practice under my belt, and I couldn't convince other doctors that I was having a heart problem. Believe me, from that point on I began to listen to my patients a lot more carefully."

In the Vietnam MASH units, the diagnosis of patients' problems was obvious   belly wound, chest wound, etc. Due to the extreme rate of wounded and casualties caused by war, their work could be more likened to an assembly line, often operating day and night. There wasn't a lot of conversation between surgeons and patients.

"Those soldiers had serious problems, and our job was to fix those problems, and quickly. Now, my job was not just to repair and heal my patients, it was to listen, and learn."

* * *

Meanwhile, Dick became more and more confident at the helm of his sailboat.

"I learned to get the damned boat out of the slip and down the bay, and what have you. We named her "Bea Hive," because of our very large family/crew. Before long, we felt we were ready for our first eighteen-hour sailing voyage to Catalina in our Columbia 36, with its little two-cylinder diesel engine.

"We came chugging in at two or three knots, at night, because I'm a night traveler, and learned a long time ago that driving, whether in a car or a boat, was easier with the children sleeping. Well, we completely missed the island. Gina was sicker than a dog, and Maria was, too. It was an absolute fiasco, a nightmare.

"Of course, Bea's furious at me. Half way up the backside of the island we realize Catalina is on my right, and it should be on my left.

"The whole time we're towing this little Sabot sailboat as our tender, our dinghy. I finally found the anchorage and we putted in. The harbormaster yelled at us to pick up a mooring just down the way.

"Well, here we are, after eighteen hours on the water with seven people—five kids aged one to ten—on this damned boat, towing the little Sabot, and nobody had ever picked up a mooring before. What the hell does that mean? I looked at Bea, she looked at me.

"So we're put-put-putting down this narrow little finger, between all these expensive yachts, and this guy decides to swim in front of us. I didn't have any choice but to stop. At that moment all hell broke loose. I threw the engine in reverse but I hadn't pulled in the line towing the Sabot. Wouldn't you know it, the towline got hung up in the prop, and we no longer had auxiliary power.

"Now we've got no power and the boat is swinging around. The Harbor Police finally came out and helped us as people on the endangered boats nearby were doing a Chinese fire drill by hanging off their boats, trying to fend off this idiot towing a Sabot that was banging into everything.

"Of course, Bea's livid with me. She yells, 'I'm going home. Get me an airplane. I've never been so embarrassed in my whole life. You bring us out here; you don't know what the heck you're doing . . .' Meanwhile, the kids are seasick and crying. It was awful.

"Well, she wouldn't talk to me the rest of the day, and wouldn't even come up on deck. The Harbor Police finally towed us to a dock, and I dove in and cut the painter line to the Sabot with my knife and freed the propeller. Fortunately, there was no permanent damage to the prop.

"Of course, in the process, the leeboard (steerage) fitting on the Sabot broke and went in the water. So we had this dinghy but couldn't sail or steer her.

"We were on our first day of what was supposed to be a month of fun in the sun, with my loving family surrounding me. All my dreams of having a nice peaceful time, sunset sails . . . it was all blowing up in my face.

"And all around us the other boaters in the anchorage just stared at us like we were the craziest boaters they had ever seen. And I'm sure we were. They were looking at us and shaking their heads as if to say, 'Here come the Griswolds.'

"One of the funniest sights must have been all seven of us gingerly trying to step down and into our five-foot Sabot to go ashore, and in front of an audience that consisted of the entire anchorage. The only thing missing was our German shepherd.

"Fortunately, in three or four days everything settled down, and we had some wonderful treks around the island and found some beautiful anchorages and moorings. It was a very pleasant month. Thank God we can laugh about it now."

* * *

Another of the more memorable Virgilio adventures came when Dick rented a motor home to take all the kids to Lake Tahoe.

"I wanted to teach them to snow ski. The problem was that none of us had ever skied. Just like none of us had ever sailed a sailboat."

The ski trip turned out to be a major success, despite nearly getting arrested for leaving three-year-old Gina, the youngest, in the motor home with the dog, while the rest of the family took ski lessons.

"Hell, I don't even buy green bananas."

From then on, for the next 15 years, every winter the Virgilio family would do two or three ski vacations. That led to their investing in timeshares in Lake Tahoe, and creating dozens and dozens of wonderful family memories along the way.

"I know I keep coming back to this, but I've never told anyone just how frightened I was, all the time. Once I had the heart surgery, and then had various repeat incidents, I felt I was living on borrowed time.

"Hell, to this day I don't even buy green bananas. I wake up in the morning and go to bed at night scared. I never know when something is going to go wrong again with my heart.

"The skiing? Well, I had no business being up in that elevation and physically exerting myself to such a degree. I felt vulnerable for the first time in my life, but I wasn't going to let that stop me from enjoying my family, whether it meant skiing, sailing, scuba diving or whatever. I knew I'd rather die with my family, living life to the fullest, than as a couch potato."

THIRTEEN

It's Not Far Down to Paradise

It had been a pretty incredible year for Dick Virgilio. His navy career was winding down and he had gone into private practice. He had a heart bypass, had his fifth child . . . and he bought a boat.

The motivator throughout was his heart. Once Dick realized there was a problem, and even though doctors finally repaired it, he was told he might not live another ten years. That scared the hell out of him.

Going into the heart surgery, all he could think about was that he wanted to spend less time being a doctor, and more time with his family. The boat just might be the key to this, he thought.

"As a kid I couldn't get enough of Captain Troy on his schooner Tiki (*Adventures in Paradise*), or of actor Jeff Chandler carousing about in the South Pacific (*Bird of Paradise*).

"I always dreamed of having a South Pacific experience of my own. But I was sure it was just that, a dream. If dreams are bucket lists, then I started my list way back when I was a kid living in Baltimore.

"Lying there in the hospital bed, wondering if I was going to awaken after surgery, I began to realize that this boat could be just the ticket. It could be the tie that binds — a way for my family and I to spend quality time together, away from work and away from other people.

"All I could think about was getting far, far away with my family. Could the boat be the vehicle to help us do that? Possibly, but that whole concept of just sailing away was so new, so fresh for me to wrap my head around. All I really knew was that we just had to all be together."

Meanwhile, at work, Dick began to notice as family values disappeared among his fellow doctors. Alcohol abuse was up and marriages began to fall apart. The excessive drinking that seemed to come with the territory wasn't a solution to their woes. On the contrary, it was the beginning of the end for many of them.

"I don't think I'd have been married today if I hadn't have gotten away from that and focused on doing things as a family.

"The two traditions that we initiated right away as a family were that we learned to snow ski and do family ski vacations; then we started taking a month every summer and going somewhere on the boat.

"The other thing was, when you take thirty days off, it's like owning your own shop. You don't get paid when you're not there. And there is always some guy behind you who does what you do, and he's just waiting for you to move aside so he can jump in and take your job.

"I wasn't even sure I was going to wake up in the morning."

"I was getting to the point where I just didn't care any longer. It wasn't as though I was making that much money, and I didn't think I was going to be around that long anyway, what with the unexpected heart issues and all. So I just felt, 'Ah, the hell with it.'

"You have to realize, there were days when I wasn't even sure I was going to wake up in the morning."

* * *

Throughout the next couple of years, 1976-77, the Virgilios got to know their boat and became more and more confident as sailors. They began to build one family experience together after another, whether it was on the ski slopes or the ocean.

Always, however, in the back of Dick's mind, the comparisons to his own, lonely childhood continued to creep into his head. He was constantly evaluating and re-evaluating his role as father and husband. "Am I doing this right? Am I a good father?"

Dick worried about this. He never seemed to find that "good father" handbook. No, he wrote it. Confident of only one thing, that he didn't want to be like his father, he moved forward year after year, striving to do more, and to be more as a father.

Eventually he realized that it wasn't about being a good father or a bad father. It was about love, and about spending as much time with your family as you could—about sharing experiences together.

And, sometimes, it might even include a solo sail on the evening breeze to collect his thoughts and pull back the arrow in the bow, before once again letting it fly.

"There were days when I first got into sailing that I just wanted to go sail in the peace and quiet of the wind. But when you've got five kids aged three to eleven, that solo sail becomes more and more elusive. My kids wanted to be going somewhere and doing something all the time.

"Typically, we'd go to Coronado and anchor in Glorietta Bay. Right away all the water toys would go in the water. Okay, so I didn't really get to sail much because I knew it was uninteresting for the children, and I didn't want them to be bored.

"The last thing I wanted was for them to say, 'Oh, God, do we have to go down and go out on that boat again?'

"So, every time we went out, we tried to make it a fun thing for them—for every little amount of time we spent on the water, we had a plan, a destination: Drop anchor, play time, back on the boat, come home, get a hamburger. You know, it was just one of those deals where the better plan you put in place the more fun everyone seemed to have.

"As they got older, the kids would bring their friends along, so they wouldn't be confined to playing with the little ones all the time.

"We spent a lot of time in Coronado, anchored on the bay side of the Silver Strand, or at Stingray Point in Glorietta Bay, and it just became our new way of life."

"Eventually we were all hooked on the sailing and the great family adventures the boat allowed us to create. In fact, every year, for the next twenty years, we never missed a three- or four-week vacation to Catalina on our boat.

"But the more we used that thirty-six-foot boat, the more we realized just how small and slow it was—and it was painfully slow.

* * *

"I had done one boat race in the Columbia 36, *Bea Hive*. It was the Newport to Ensenada Race, and it was memorable for all the wrong reasons.

"I talked five other doctors into being part of our racing team. Now, you have to realize, these were five doctors who didn't know shit about sailing—never flown a spinnaker, hardly knew port from starboard.

"We took off from Newport, sailing the outside course of the Coronado Islands, and dead reckoning because we had no navigation gear back then. We were doing really badly. Nobody else had a spinnaker up, and we couldn't figure out why, so we put ours up, thinking that would help.

"Well, the reason nobody had them up is because we were sailing on a close reach, and it was blowing pretty strong.

"I had a little alcohol stove down below, and I went down to make dinner. Just as I lit the stove, the spinnaker caught a blast of air, the boat took a knock down and the alcohol spilled all over my pants. Of course, I couldn't see it, because alcohol flames are practically invisible.

"For chrissake, Virgilio's gone off his rocker. He's gone crazy."

"All of a sudden, I looked down and my pant leg was on fire. And the boat was still on its side. Well, I flew out of that salon, through the cockpit, and jumped overboard in the hope the saltwater would put out the fire on my leg. And, no, I wasn't wearing a life vest.

"Fortunately, I grabbed a stanchion as I went over because, despite the panic of seeing my leg on fire, I had an equally frightful thought that none of these doctors knew how to pick up a man overboard, right the boat, or even turn the boat around, for that matter.

"It was hysterical. None of the crew could see the fire on my leg because it was an alcohol flame, and had no idea why I had run out of the salon and jumped overboard. I remember hearing one of them say, 'For chrissake, Virgilio's gone off his rocker. He's gone crazy.'

"We finally made it to Ensenada. I had planned to take my crew out to dinner when we arrived, but, because my pants were burnt and wet, I hung them on the lifeline to dry out. I had forgotten I had $300 in my pants pocket.

"Well, by the time we realized it, you could see all this paper currency flying through the air and floating in our wake. I mean it was the biggest disaster you could ever imagine, but that was my first competitive experience."

* * *

The San Diego Yacht Club, where Dick was a member, is what might be described as a very sophisticated club. After Dick's Newport to Ensenada Race, word traveled fast that he might not be the most ideal crewmember to invite on your boat. In fact, no one would invite him to race on their boats for a very long time.

Dick knew the only way he was going to be able to compete in the racing venue at the yacht club was to purchase his own competitive boat. So, in 1977, he traded in the Bea Hive on an Erickson 39, a boat with a proven race record.

"Even though it was only a few feet longer, the Erickson 39 seemed really big compared to what we had been sailing, and faster. It had a four-cylinder, rather than a two-cylinder engine, and that's about the time I decided to get into racing."

* * *

Yacht clubs can be cliquish, especially to new members, but Dick persisted. After three boats, he finally owned a vessel that, with the right hands at the helm, could be competitive.

Yacht racing, as in most sports, finds participants always looking for that little extra edge—that little something that will make them run faster or jump higher. In Dick's case, his mission was simply to sail better. Dick joined the Erikson 39 Association and began to make new friends.

He had come into the yacht racing game so late in life he really wasn't looking for a "ringer" as much as he was looking to learn, to gain knowledge from the best there was. He found that in young racing phenom, Robbie Haines, a future Olympic gold medal sailor.

At the time, Robbie and his crew—Rod Davis and Eddie Trevelyan—were the hottest things on the water. They sailed out of Coronado Yacht Club, where Dick had spent a lot of time and had gotten to know them.

"Robbie and I had become friends over the years, so I asked him to help me."

They began to campaign Dick's boat and soon won the Erikson 39 nationals.

"Everyone at the yacht club was mad at me because I had introduced professional sailors into the game. Now, of course, everyone uses hired guns to campaign their boats."

Eventually, Haines, Davis, and Trevelyan would go on to win seven world championships in four different boat classes. They were awarded the Congressional Gold Medal for being a member of the 1980 U.S. Olympic Sailing Team, which did not compete in the Soviet Union because of a boycott of the Games that year, signed by then-President Jimmy Carter.

Then, at the 1984 Los Angeles Summer Olympics, the boys finally earned their gold medal in the Soling Class, going down in history as three of the greatest sailors to ever come out of San Diego area.

With that sort of fame came more offers. The three young sailors would go on to compete, as well as work as hired guns, on many famous boats, with many famous skippers. Roy E. Disney was one of the wealthy members of the sailing community who wanted to win (nephew to Walt Disney and heir to the Magic Kingdom), no matter what the cost. Disney made Haines a regular part of his afterguard early on.

"We had a lot of fun campaigning that Erikson," Dick said. "Then one day Robbie came to me and said, 'You know, Dr. Virgilio, we need to get you a real racing boat, a Peterson two-ton.'

"Well, I wasn't sure how to react to that. I told him I was just a humble Navy veteran, barely getting by on $35,000 a year. How on earth was I going to afford a $130,000 boat?

"Robbie said he knew the designer, Doug Peterson, and that he would talk to him, and maybe get me a break on the design fee, among other things.

"The next thing I know, I'm sitting at a conference table in the San Diego Yacht Club board room with Carl Eichenlaub, Nick Frazee, and a couple of other major players in the yachting industry."

At that time, Nick Frazee had recently purchased Eichenlaub Yachts, the legendary boatyard located on Shelter Island, that was currently building all the hot new racing boats and downwind sleds. Doug Peterson would design the boats and Carl would build them.

"Eichenlaub didn't have any boats in the yard at the moment, and he agreed to build it. So here I am, this navy commander making peanuts, sitting at the table with all these waterfront legends, and setting in motion the design and construction of an expensive racing boat that I had no money to pay for.

"They said, 'Well, here's the deal. You give us your Erikson 39 and we'll take care of getting rid of that as your down payment on this boat. Now, you're a doctor, right? Fine. Just go see our friend Bob over at the Bank of America, and he'll loan you the money right away. Give Carl a $5,000 deposit and he'll have you a new boat in six weeks. And you don't have to worry about a thing.'

"What a good ol' boys' network these guys had. I was amazed. In fact, it all happened so rapidly that I signed the contract, stood up from the table, and I was dizzy. And then I had this horrible thought that Bea didn't know anything about any of this . . . yet.

"Well, I didn't have $200 in my checking account, but I tried to be very suave about it all and wrote a check for $5,000 to Carl Eichenlaub. As he took the check, I leaned over and whispered to Carl there was no money in my account to cover that check.

"He looked at me and said, 'Don't worry about it. I'll hold on to the check and won't cash it until you get the loan.' I went to the bank and Bob Jaundall was expecting me. He already knew Carl was building me a boat. He said he would give me a $120,000 line of credit and told me to start saving my money for those future payments."

Bea: "You have got to be kidding me."

Dick began spending lots of time down at the Eichenlaub Boat-yard, watching him build this amazing boat from nothing—from the ground up.

Bea was beginning to wonder where he was all the time, so he knew he would finally have to tell her. One day he got up his nerve and just blurted it out:

Dick: "By the way, Bea, honey, we're going to get rid of the Erickson 39—Free Spirit."

Bea: "Why? I love that boat."

Dick: "I know, but I have a great opportunity here."

The right words didn't come easily. He was stalling and stammering, so he finally just blurted out that he had bought this boat that they couldn't afford, with a promise to pay it off the next year.

It was obvious to Dick none of this was working for Bea, so he tried to smooth out the damaged confession by mentioning that Robbie Haines, the famous Olympic medalist, was going to be the project manager, and that he would race the new boat with them, and they could sell it for a profit. A profit!

Bea: "You have got to be kidding me."

As the boat began to take shape on Shelter Island, Eichenlaub told Dick to order sails for the boat. Again, Dick had to scratch his head. He simply didn't have money for sails. He went back to the bank and explained his predicament to Jaundall. The banker told him not to worry, that he would just raise the line of credit another $20,000. He assured Dick that nothing was going to happen until the whole project was finished.

"And damn if Carl didn't do that for me. He built that whole boat and never took a dime out of my line of credit. He knew it was there, his shop wasn't doing that well, and yet he gave that boat the best he had to offer."

Dick never asked, but he was pretty sure that Frazee, the new owner of the Eichenlaub Boatyard, was never made aware of the details of his "good old boys" deal between the bank, the designers, and builders.

Several years later, Dick and another partner bought Nick Frazee's celebrated 70-foot downwind sled, Swiftsure. Nick Frazee and Dick Virgilio became good friends and remained close for the rest of Nick's life.

Nick Frazee passed on April 2, 2017, while this book was being written. Dick Virgilio was with him when he passed. In Dick's words:

"I will always feel extremely fortunate to have had Nick as a friend. He was a loving husband, father, and a true friend to many of us in Point Loma. His devotion and loyalty to his family inspired his friends to be better people. I think of him daily, and miss him dearly."

* * *

It's been said that a boat is just a hole in the water into which you

Dick and Robbie Haines heading out to race Dick's newly commissioned Peterson two-ton, Volare.

Volare *racing in the waters off San Diego*

pour money. It's also been said the happiest times for a boat owner are the day he buys his boat, and the day he sells it. Dick had his boat. He had sails. But he had no rigging.

"Somewhere along the line I met this guy, Gary Faulk. He had sailed on my Erikson 39 and was a rigger. He told me I ought to have my own rigging company. I think my reaction was, 'Huh?'"

"Well, after he explained what rigging would cost me, and put my options on the table, he convinced me that owning my own rigging company would allow me to rig my boat wholesale, make money on other boats, and write the whole thing off.

"So we opened Sunset Rigging. We bought a VW van and had 'Sunset Rigging' printed all over it. I talked my good friend Dr. Fred Frye into coming in on the deal with me."

About this time, word began to travel around the Shelter Island boating community that Eichenlaub was about to launch his latest creation.

"In those days, Eichenlaub Boatyard couldn't launch that big of a boat, so we hired a boat mover to move it to Driscoll's yard, just down the road a piece.

"It was like a funeral procession. Me, Bea, the five kids, all walking very slowly down Shelter Island Drive. It seemed like all of Point Loma turned out to watch this procession. You could hear them talking, 'Who owned this boat? Who's this Virgilio guy?'

"We named the boat Volare, which means 'to fly' in Italian. When we christened her at Driscoll's yard, Carl came up to me, smiling. He says, 'Here, I've got something for you.' It was my check for the initial $5,000. What a great guy he was.

"Meanwhile, we went out and got a bottle of champagne to christen the boat. Bea whacked the bow of the boat three times, until a piece of my new, very expensive bow broke off. Finally she hit a piece of aluminum and the bottle broke. Nobody had told us there were special bottles used to christen boats. But that was my introduction into really sophisticated racing.

"I probably wasn't any better a sailor than I was that first day on the water, but I just happened to get involved with great people like Robbie Haines, Eddie Trevelyan, Carl Eichenlaub, Doug Peterson, and Nick Frazee.

"There was a little something in it for all of us. Carl got paid to build a boat, Doug for his design. Robbie and Eddie used this experience to move up into larger boats and faster races, and I got my new 'family' boat and, even though it was built for speed rather than comfort, it was still our family boat. I had Volare fitted out for minimal comfort and she was finished in time for us to make our annual Catalina pilgrimage on her.

"I had been good about working odd jobs and saving money for future loan payments. Our goal was to make this boat worth something so that I could sell it within twelve months and, hopefully, make a profit, although, in hindsight, who ever makes a profit on a boat?

"To raise the boat's profile, we competed (and did very well) in a number of races. Well, Robbie did well, I should say. I just watched, listened, and learned everything I could from him.

"We raced the San Diego to Ensenada Race, Newport-Ensenada Race, the Newport-Cabo San Lucas Race, and just about everything between San Diego and Los Angeles. We had built quite a reputation on the yacht-racing scene for ourselves.

"The Acapulco Challenge involved the best and richest Mexican yacht racers. They would all come to San Diego, where we would then switch boats and compete in a round-robin elimination. The race would alternate each year between San Diego and Acapulco. As Volare's owner, and on the newest and most provocative two-tonner on the water, I was asked to participate.

"I was about to own a boat, free and clear, for the first time in my life"

"As fate would have it, Jorge Escalante, a very wealthy yacht racer from Acapulco, fell in love with my boat. He ended up buying her for

$200,000. The deal closed and I had the cash a week before I was due to start paying off the bank loan.

* * *

"The year before, I had raced in the Acapulco Challenge. While in Acapulco, I had seen a cherry Cal 40 moored at the yacht club. I asked who owned it and was told that Jorge Escalante was the owner.

"At the time, the Cal 40 was a favorite racing boat of the Trans-Pac fleet, and a couple of Cal 40s had even won that famous race. We made the Cal 40 part of the deal, delivered to San Diego, of course. I was about to own a boat, free and clear, for the first time in my life.

"Unfortunately, the Cal 40 that I had seen in Acapulco was not the one owned by Jorge. Something, apparently, was lost in translation. When it finally arrived in San Diego, it was in such bad shape that you had to take a shower after going down below.

"Bea and the children couldn't believe that I had given up our beautiful yacht for this piece of shit. However, after I had her gutted and rebuilt from the inside out, they realized what a beautiful boat the Cal 40 was. We kept the name Volare, and she turned out to be a real nice boat, a very nice looking and sailing boat. She hosted us on many a great sailing day in San Diego and Catalina.

"Looking back now, and remembering all we went through, you have no idea how I sweated building that two-tonner, not knowing how I was going to pay for her. Several years later, we sold the Cal 40 to a couple in Los Angeles for $60,000, which was a lot of money for a Cal 40 in those days.

"I essentially went through five boats in five years. About that time, Jack Kelly and Doug Peterson came out with their Kelly-Peterson 46 and I put in an order for hull number six.

"The boat was delivered in the late summer of 1983, and we named her Bravo. We would have that boat for the next fourteen years, making some wonderful cruises to Hawaii and the South Pacific, and all the way to Australia.

* * *

"I had been thinking about long-range cruising with the family for quite some time, and these new forty-six-footers seemed perfect for what I wanted to do from that point forward—to do my Jeff Chandler and Captain Troy thing in the South Pacific.

"As the summer of 1984 approached, I laid out a plan for the family and our new boat. I told them that we were going to cruise to San Francisco for the summer.

"Keep in mind, our longest trip prior to that, as a family, was an eight-hour trip to Catalina. I'm sure that was a lot for them to swallow, but we made the trip north along the coast to San Francisco. Winds are contrary for that leg of the journey, so we motored most of the way.

"I researched the heck out of this trip. Prior to our departure, I asked my partner at the time, Ben Gibbs, to fly me up the coast so I could photograph the anchorages and marinas we might pull into on our journey.

"I planned the trip so that the longest leg was actually San Diego to Catalina. That was a distance that I knew the family could tolerate.

"I also planned only one-night passages, again, so the family could enjoy the days in different anchorages and ports while I slept.

"We made stops in Santa Cruz Island, Santa Barbara, Point Conception, Avila Beach, Morro Bay, San Simeon, and along the coast of Big Sur to Monterey, Santa Cruz, San Francisco, and all the way up the Delta to Tinsley Island, where the Saint Francis Yacht Club had an out station.

"While in Catalina for our first stopover, I learned of my mother's death in Baltimore. I can't recall how my secretary contacted me, but she was able to find us, and I had to make a decision whether to leave Bea and the kids in Catalina with the boat and fly back by myself for her funeral, or to bring the boat back to San Diego and take the entire family back to Baltimore.

"Because of the delay in finding us, however, the funeral was already scheduled, and I was going to have to get to the East Coast within the next two days.

"It was a very difficult decision to make, but I decided to fly back alone, and leave Bea and the children with the boat on Catalina. Of course, I had complete confidence in them to take care of the boat while I was gone. To this day, however, I regret that I didn't take them back with me to pay our final respects to my mother, together, as a family.

"I returned as soon as I could, and we rejoined our itinerary from Catalina. I'll never forget slipping under that Golden Gate Bridge at the helm of my own boat. It was such a wonderful feeling of accomplishment for me, and something I had wanted to do my entire life—another bucket list item checked off, and, yes, that was the highlight of the trip for me."

The Virgilios spent quite a bit of time in the Bay Area, motoring on the Delta and up to Tiburon and Tinsley Island—sailing whenever the winds were favorable.

As summer drew to a close, the two oldest children, Maria and Angela, flew home with Bea to prepare for college. Dick and the other three children, ages ten, twelve, and fourteen, readied the boat to travel once more, then brought her back down the coast. This time there would be very little motoring, as prevailing winds did the trick.

Storms around Point Conception gave them a challenge or two but by then the Virgilio children had become excellent crew. As a reward, Dick pulled into Catalina on the way home and gave his kids a chance to have a last fling before school started. It was one heck of a way to end 1984.

* * *

It seems there's always one more mountain to climb. For Dick that next mountain was his dream to sail to Hawaii. He had made the trip to San Francisco, sailed to Ensenada, twice to Manzanillo. He had a decade of boating experience behind him at that point.

Was it possible he might actually realize his childhood dream of sailing the South Pacific? A sail to Hawaii seemed the only natural progression in this new world of the Virgilio family. Shades of Jeff Chandler and Captain Troy....

FOURTEEN

The Birth of the San Diego Trauma System

Life was not all about port and starboard tacks. It's important to look back to the year 1974 to understand the stress that drove Dick Virgilio to the water, to realize the depth of his dedication to medicine and saving lives.

At that time, Dick was enjoying his repaired heart and discovering the world of boating. He had been mulling a situation at work that just didn't sit right with him—the lack of timely and proper trauma care in San Diego hospitals.

Perhaps it was just the accumulation of information he had been collecting in his brain since returning from Vietnam, but he began to compare trauma care on the battlefield to patient care in civilian hospitals. He began to see how terribly lacking medical care of acute trauma was in San Diego.

"It weighed heavily on me. One of our young navy personnel would get in an accident and would be taken to the nearest hospital. That hospital would then have to notify us that they had one of ours. Or, worse, they would fail to notify us and try to treat the patient in their facility, which wasn't equipped to handle severely injured patients.

"This really bothered me, as precious time was lost in the process, time that could lead to death, and often did. Something had to be done. So I took one of our old ambulances and outfitted it with a respirator. Then we added everything else we might need to turn that ambulance into a mobile, mini-MASH unit.

"You could put a medical team in that thing, run down to Bay General Hospital, pull the patient out, and, even if he was on a ventilator, we could bring him back to Balboa and take care of him.

"All of my moonlighting work in local emergency rooms allowed me to witness firsthand how difficult it was for the system to adequately care for severely injured patients.

"No matter how qualified an emergency room doctor was, if he didn't have immediate surgical and operating room backup, the result was going to be a dead patient. And most of the time, these deaths could be characterized as preventable.

"You had a better chance of surviving a gunshot wound in the jungles of Vietnam than a car accident in San Diego."

"I was so upset with the kind of care that some of these people were getting, I decided to do something about it. One day I just couldn't take it any longer. After one of our guys died at one of the other hospitals, I got on my soapbox and made a statement in the local press.

"It was no exaggeration when I said back then that, 'You had a better chance of surviving a gunshot wound in the jungles of Vietnam than a car accident in San Diego.'

"It ran in the newspaper, and for a time I was the bad guy on the block. It appeared to my contemporaries that I was badmouthing medical care in San Diego, which was supposed to be the modern hub of medicine.

"But I rocked the medical establishment pretty good, and that's the reason we have such a fantastic trauma system here now. Not just because of me, but because we stirred up a lot of dust and got a lot of folks' attention. Suddenly people were talking about preventable deaths, as opposed to non-preventable deaths."

Dick's modesty doesn't do justice to the changes his efforts brought about in San Diego medicine. To this day, Dr. Dick Virgilio is known as the father of the San Diego trauma system. Countless lives have been saved, and are still being saved because of Dick's dedication to his craft, his determination to do his job better, and to raise the bar in area hospitals.

At that time, there were no trauma centers in San Diego, except the small unit Dick had created at Balboa Hospital, and it wasn't hooked into the community—to the Emergency Medical Services (EMS) system in the community.

Based on the same theory that introduced MASH units experimenting near the front lines in Korea, and evolving even more in Vietnam, Dick and his team began to raise awareness throughout the San Diego County medical community that, "time was of the essence," when dealing with critically injured patients.

The message Dick and his fellow surgeons were trying to get across was simple: Taking a badly injured patient to the nearest hospital was not the answer. For the best results, the patient had to be taken to the nearest "appropriate" hospital. The optimum word being, appropriate.

"There were no protocols on what patients went to what hospitals. Trauma patients were taken to the nearest hospital that had an emergency room. Again, the problem was that just one doctor was all too often the only person staffing emergency rooms. And that doctor, unfortunately, was not trained to treat trauma patients.

"That doctor had no immediate surgical backup and would have to start calling in surgeons from a list posted on the wall, which resulted in delays in decisive treatment and, more often than not, a preventable death.

"Not only was there undo delay in getting in sufficient surgical backup, but these delays crossed over into anesthesia, operating room personnel, radiology, pathology, and touching on just about every department in the hospital.

"What was needed was to change the concept that the nearest hospital was the best choice in such situations.

"The public, and specifically the medical community, had to be educated on this. They had to accept the validity of designating a few larger hospitals throughout the county as trauma centers.

"These centers would have to have twenty-four-hour, in-house surgical, anesthesia, and operating room coverage so that delays in treatment could be minimized."

Dick's observations, because of his personal experiences at so many area hospitals, gave him a unique perspective. That, combined with his MASH experiences, made him the perfect candidate to push for reform within the system. It was not an easy sell, and Dick would have his work cut out for him in the wake of his leaving the navy.

* * *

In 1978, Dick retired from the navy. He took a part-time position as head of the surgical intensive care unit at Mercy Hospital in San Diego. In addition, he began to assist one of the more popular and successful heart surgeons in the area, Dr. Leland Housman, who also worked out of Mercy Hospital. Ironically, Dr. Housman would perform two heart surgeries on Dick in the months and years to come.

Dick eventually started his own private practice, as a vascular surgeon. He never gave up, however, on the idea of improving care for the severely injured people of San Diego County.

He never ceased to talk up the benefits of properly outfitted hospitals in dealing with trauma patients. For a time, he was the only candle in what seemed like a large and very dark room, yet he continued to lecture, not only across the county but the country, on trauma care, raising the bar of awareness and acceptance a little more each time.

What he discovered quickly was that he had to find a way to teach without criticizing, to educate without alienating his fellow doctors along the way. No one likes to be told how to do their jobs, least of all doctors.

Finally, Dick Virgilio, Brent Eastman, and a couple of other people convinced the San Diego County Board of Supervisors to fund a study on preventable deaths from trauma in San Diego County. The resulting figures were staggering.

"We went around and got all the medical records we could, but it wasn't easy. Personal medical records are a sensitive thing, and if not handled correctly could result in lawsuits. So all of this research had to be done without the patients' names—just looking at the medical data available.

"The question boiled down to, 'Should this patient have lived or died?'

"The thing about operating on trauma patients is that you can always just blame the circumstance that brought them in for your failure to save the patient—the automobile or the motorcycle; the gunshot wound, or whatever. And many doctors did just that.

"I mean, somebody comes in all crunched up after an automobile accident and dies. Well, that's all right because it was the car's fault. It was the accident's fault.

"A third of patient deaths could have been prevented."

"The truth is that a certain percentage of those patients who died should have lived, and they would have, had they had access to immediate care by a surgeon and an anesthesiologist—a trauma team put together that's in a specific location twenty-four/seven, always there, always ready to intervene.

"Our research showed that about a third of patient deaths could have been prevented.

"Now, keep in mind, this wasn't because the doctor who saw the patient was bad. It was because the system was bad. There was too much pressure put on doctors and hospitals because the process itself was flawed.

"The rule was, you had to take a patient to the nearest hospital, whether that facility had the necessary in-house staff to adequately treat the patient, or not.

"I was a good trauma surgeon, but I couldn't do it all by myself. I can remember times when I was alone, moonlighting in local emergency rooms, when I'd have my finger on someone's aorta to stop the bleeding, and my other hand on the phone trying to get a doctor with surgical privileges to come in and operate on the patient.

"Shit, you just don't have time for that. You've got to have a team in place, waiting to pounce on that patient when he comes in. You've got to have backup, no matter how good you are. If not, you're going to have a patient die when he should've stayed alive, and that was the crux of my concerns as it pertained to trauma surgery in San Diego."

* * *

As a result of greater attention to the issue, and armed with the survey findings, terms like "qualified locations" and "trauma centers" began to seep into local nomenclature when dealing with trauma patients.

Word travelled fast of Dick Virgilio's efforts to bring change to trauma care in San Diego. Numerous other medical facilities soon were applying to become qualified trauma centers.

Eventually, an independent committee from the American College of Surgeons came out and inspected those facilities that had submitted proposals for consideration.

Before long, accepted criteria was put in place defining Level One and Level Two trauma-care centers. In 1984 the San Diego County Trauma System was officially inaugurated. The five hospitals selected to participate were Mercy, UCSD, Sharp, Scripps La Jolla, and Palomar. It was the dawn of a new era in medical treatment for trauma patients in San Diego. Lives were being saved!

* * *

A year prior to the birth of the trauma system, Dick had experienced a second heart attack, which caused him to reassess his life yet again.

"For the first time, I was really excited about the future, but, after owning the boat for just a few months, I experienced a reality check in the form of my second heart attack. Suddenly, I was facing yet another heart operation.

"I guess I had known there were problems, but I didn't want to accept that. I was in denial about my tiredness and chest pains, and, looking back now, I suppose I was afraid to accept that I might be having another heart incident. If you've never been through one, you can't imagine how that can work on your mind.

"This time they did the angiogram right away. It showed that the grafts put in twelve years earlier were occluding—closing up, shutting down. I was forty-eight at that point. The grafts were put in when I was thirty-six."

"Get the operating room ready!"

The cardiologist instructed Dick on the situation, and what lay ahead for him if he did the second heart surgery. He explained that Dick didn't need to do this operation; he could just change his life—eat better, tone down his vacations, and stress level and, as Dick feared, enjoy the remainder of his life on the couch watching TV.

"I had been working with a fellow heart surgeon, Dr. Lee Houseman for years. He knew everything I had been through, so I called him at 10 p.m. that night and told him to get the operating room ready."

More than anyone, Dick knew that the mortality rate from a second or third open-heart surgery increased exponentially due to the difficulty of accessing the heart—what with all the scar tissue that sets up after each surgery. Dick laughs now at the comedy of errors that ensued in getting him to the hospital that night.

"I'm waiting for Bea to get dressed to drive me to the hospital. I'm waiting, and waiting, and waiting. Finally, I yelled at her, 'Fer chrissake, Bea, I've got to get in there.'

"She said something about figuring out what to wear, and what to do, and this and that. Of course, she denies it today, but she actually said to me, 'Hey, it's easy for you to say; you're going to be asleep on the operating table. I'm going to be in the waiting room the next morning when everyone comes in to see how you are doing.' "

In Bea's defense, it had to be quite a shock to have her husband roll over in bed and say he was having a heart attack. It's not uncommon for a jolt like that to create confusion of priorities, and make chaos out of routine.

Once at the hospital, everyone began to calm down. Dick knew all the nurses and doctors in the operating room, so it was like home for him. His team comprised the best players possible—the most qualified medical specialists Dick knew—and that was saying something.

While some suggested he go to the Mayo Clinic and assemble the best medical team possible, Dick refused, saying, he wanted to stay there, where he knew everybody. Such was his faith in that medical team. Surely his faith was their concern. No one wanted to lose the good Dr. Virgilio on their watch.

"They took out the other veins—the vein grafts that had occluded—and replaced them with newer ones. In those days they only used vein grafts from your leg. The process involves bypassing—hooking the new vein to the aorta, creating an artery beyond the blockage, which is why it's called a bypass operation."

* * *

Dick had been offered the position of trauma director at Mercy Hospital prior to having the heart attack and bypass surgery. With the uncertainty of his heart condition, and his desire to spend more time with his family, he politely turned down the offer.

Mercy was poised to become a benchmark trauma program, but

apparently not with Dick Virgilio at the helm. At the time, Sister M. Joanne Devincenti was the CEO of Mercy and a good friend of Dick's, which made the decision even more difficult for him.

"While I was recovering in the hospital, my secretary, Suzanne, visited me. She had been going over some business stuff and said she had some bad news. She said my medical insurance was all screwed up. Essentially, she said I had no medical insurance at all.

"How that happened, I don't know. But Suzanne went on to say that she had received my first bill from this recent heart surgery, and that it was about $100,000.

"Well, that nearly put me in for a third heart attack, but when I got on my feet I paid Sister Joanne a visit. I told the Sister that I had reconsidered taking over their trauma center.

"She asked what made me come to my senses. I laid the bill down on her desk and told her I would take over her trauma center if she tore up my heart surgery bill and threw it away. She did.

"Sister Joanne was such a neat gal, and now we were in partnership together, about to run this much-needed, and long-awaited trauma center at Mercy Hospital. Of course, she paid me well in that position, and tearing up my medical bill was sort of a gesture of good will on her part, not unlike a bonus."

* * *

Even though he knew it would require a lot of time and effort, Dick's desire to bring quality trauma care to San Diego outweighed any other considerations. He accepted the position.

At the time, administrators at Mercy had no idea they were poised to become a benchmark trauma program that would inspire other hospitals to follow.

The county was divided into five catchment areas, and each of the hospitals was assigned an area. Mercy's catchment area included the south bay and the inner city.

Little did Dick know how difficult it would be to transform a quiet, carriage trade hospital such as Mercy—which specialized in catering to an affluent cliental—into an inner-city trauma center.

The hospital and the physicians were accustomed to dealing with patients who either had medical insurance or could pay cash for their services.

Suddenly the hallways were filled with tattooed, body-pierced individuals who had no idea what health insurance was, and certainly didn't have the means to pay for their care.

Many patients were admitted from, as Dick put it, "the local knife and gun clubs." Many of those were under arrest for having committed some felony. These patients had to have 24/7 police guard, thus, there were times that Mercy Hospital looked more like a prison hospital.

"Here comes Virgilio, and all his friends."

The staff, along with the Bankers Hill clientele, was stunned at these intense changes. To say the least, they were put out.

It was difficult for Dick to get the necessary backup from surgical subspecialists because of the poor pay class. He quickly became the most unpopular physician on the staff.

He can remember times when he was walking down the hall, by himself, and would hear somebody say, "Here comes Virgilio, and all his friends."

He remembers Bea getting several calls in the middle of the night, while he was working late, telling her that her husband had been severally injured and was in the ER. On one occasion, they even told her that he had been killed.

Dick would later admit that this hostility toward the creation of a trauma center at Mercy, and to him personally, really hurt. It did not, however, stop him from forging ahead with his desire to transform Mercy Hospital into the premier trauma hospital that it is today.

It took several years and many sleepless nights to negotiate contracts with the hospital that allowed Dick to adequately reimburse the sub-specialists and to put together a team of surgeons who just did trauma, and didn't have to worry about trying to balance a private practice of surgery alongside the rigors of 24-hour trauma coverage.

The staff gradually adapted to the diversity in their patient population and the hospital was well on its way to becoming one of the premier trauma centers in the country.

Until his retirement in 1996, Dick worked relentlessly to insure Mercy Hospital did its part as a Level One Trauma Center in delivering quality care to the injured people of San Diego County.

Dick's efforts to establish a trauma recovery system found him teaching the residents, and writing and publishing papers to help others in the field of medicine better understand this important area of treatment.

As he got to know more and more surgeons from around the country, he found others involved in a similar crusade to improve critical care surgery. They began to have meetings, then put together special medical conferences onboard cruise ships, of all things.

Anyone who wanted to know more about this new method of emergency medical treatment could sign on, along with their wives, for a cruise that was filled with lectures and clinics at sea—cutting edge medical information that would slowly change the world of medicine.

Gradually, the climate changed from fear of the unknown to the reality that there was indeed a better way to treat trauma patients.

In all, Dick and Bea did nine Caribbean cruises in the process of sharing the latest information on trauma care. Each voyage introduced 150 new students and doctors to this information.

There is no way to determine how many thousands of lives have been saved, and continue to be saved, because of Dick's efforts.

Because of this, Dr. Dick Virgilio owns the title, "Father of the San Diego Trauma System."

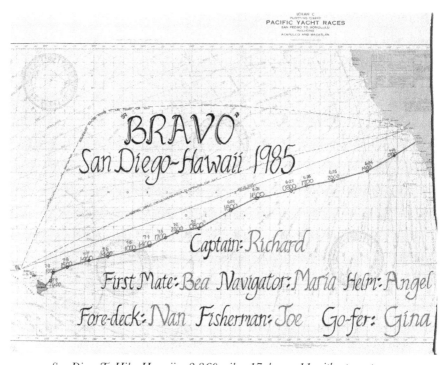

San Diego To Hilo, Hawaii – 2,360 miles, 17 days—11 without any power.

FIFTEEN

"Hawaii or Bust…or Both"

Even with so much going on in his personal and professional life, and after a second heart surgery, Dick Virgilio was ready to climb that next mountain, to check off yet another item from his bucket list.

Despite his doctor's warning of, "Don't do anything strenuous," Dick decided to sail his boat to Hawaii in search of Michener's South Pacific and childhood fantasies from watching old Jeff Chandler movies and Adventures in Paradise.

"This is how we stupid surgeons think; if we can cut and sew, then we can do anything, right? You have to know that, deep down, we're all a bunch of egomaniacs. So, one day I called my family together and told them that this has got to be. I explained that it might be a hard deal, but we were going to sail our boat to Hawaii.

"I explained that they wouldn't be able to take a lot of stuff, and that we would be at sea for probably ten days. Well, it turned out to be 17 days. But my instructions were to bring just enough to last ten days, because a boat is only so big, and less so with a family of seven.

"I assured them that their dad had everything under control, 'I'll take care of everything,' I boldly announced. 'All you've got to do is get on the boat. Oh, and please just bring one or two pairs of shoes.' I felt the latter was important because, well, you know how women are, and we had five of them in our family. Regardless of what I said, or what they heard, the day we left, there must've been forty pairs of shoes on that boat.

"That's when the fun began. My youngest daughter, Gina, saved the day. She knew where everything was on that boat. She helped find little places to shove stuff into, and was the designated gofer for the rest of the trip.

"The week before we departed, I honestly thought that I actually understood everything I needed to know about that boat and this trip.

"I mean, I had new electronics and a satellite navigation system. It didn't give you instantaneous read outs like modern day GPS systems do, but every four or five hours, the satellite would pass over us and, theoretically, we would get a fix on where we were. Or so we thought.

"I don't need a sextant."

"About a week before we left, one of my best friends, Mike Casinelli, asked me which sextant I was taking with us. Mike had navigated nearly a dozen TransPac races and was a very good sailor and navigator.

"I had all these electronic gadgets and told him I didn't need a sextant, complaining that I had too much crap on the boat as it was. Besides, I didn't know how to use the damned thing.

"Mike shook his head and invited me to his house for dinner. 'Bring the kids,' he said. Mike lived up in Cardiff-by-the-Sea, on the cliffs overlooking the Pacific Ocean.

"The first thing he did was take me out on the porch and attempt to show me how to use his sextant. 'I can't do this,' I pleaded. 'I'm dyslexic and I'm not very smart. I can't learn a whole new deal like this in just a week.' So he called Maria, my oldest, to join us out on the porch.

"He and Maria spent about two hours out there. Mike gave me his sextant and a whole stack of books with all these navigational tables in them. I figured after all he had gone through that night, that I should probably humor him. So I took the sextant and the books, and somehow we found a place on the boat to store them, out of sight of course.

"The day before our departure, another friend of mine, an orthopedic surgeon, came down and gave me a box. In it was a Japanese calculator that took all those navigational tables and reduced them to an electronic keyboard. All you had to do was put in your GMT (Greenwich Mean Time), the actual time, the body that you were shooting into, and the angle you got. I thought, boy, this is great, and proceeded to throw it down below and forget about it because I knew I wasn't going to need it either.

"The good news was that I could get rid of all the books that Mike had given me. The girls saw me removing the books and quickly filled the space with more shoes.

"I look back now and realize, if not for those two hours on Mike's porch and this loaned equipment, dumb shit Virgilio would have still been flopping hopelessly around in the Pacific, with no idea where he was.

"The day of departure came and we felt we had everything we needed on that boat, and a lot of stuff we didn't need. There was quite a bit of fanfare. Everyone came down to the dock to see us off. In Catalina, it was, 'Here come the Griswolds.' Upon our departure for Hawaii it was, 'There go the Griswolds.'

* * *

"I felt good about it. I wasn't scared or anything. I really thought I had everything under control. Then we sailed out beyond Point Loma, and I nearly ran into a barge. That night it blew like crazy out of the northwest, and we fell off our rhumb line."

The rhumb line is an imaginary line on the earth's surface representing any of the 32 points on the compass   a sailor's term for sailing a relatively straight line to navigate to their destination.

"My youngest, Gina, was so seasick I thought I was going to have to start her on IV (intravenous feeding). She was eight at the time.

Everyone was sick, even Maria, my oldest, who was eighteen. Bea and I were sick as well. I was throwing up like crazy.

"Finally, after forty-eight hours, which seemed like forever, the prevailing winds filled in and shifted around behind us. That's when the ride smoothed out and everyone began to show signs of life again. The next seven days were great.

"As things settled down, we began to get into a routine. Bea could go below and make dinners without getting sick. We had two fishing poles off the stern, but didn't catch any fish. Everyone had to pull a designated watch. Bea and I started out standing the night watches to let the kids sleep."

[Log Entry: It's now 8 p.m. on the 24th. Since my last entry in the log we have traveled 100 miles, had all sorts of weather, including 22 knots of breeze with large waves, which forced us to change from our gennaker to our staysail. At the present time, the wind has moderated and we are back with the large gennaker.]

"I thought we were doing pretty well, that things were okay. All our electronics were working. Then, without notice, the engine started heating up. I went down and found that there was a leak in the impeller. 'Well,' I said to myself, 'I know how to fix that.' So I took the impeller out and put a new one in. I put the plate back on but there was still a little drip.

"That's when the irony of ironies took place. I brought enough medical supplies to perform an appendectomy if I had to, but, ironically, I didn't have enough tools to fix a tiny impeller on the boat's engine.

"I mean, we could have lived with the little drip, but, being a surgeon, you never wanted to close up a belly when there was a little drip of blood, or you'd be back in there in no time. So I figured I had to tighten the bolts on the impeller plate. When I did, the bolts stripped, and we were doomed.

"We were clearly past the point of no return."

Without an autopilot, all hands had to steer, even little Gina.

"I had no way to get the engine started again. I couldn't charge the batteries and they started going down and down and down.

"I couldn't even start the generator and, of course, I had no extra batteries on the boat. So we went from full electronics to, within twenty-four hours, not even having a compass light or autopilot. Worse, we had no refrigeration. I was so depressed that I broke down in tears quietly by myself on the foredeck that night.

"By then we're six or seven days out, and clearly past the point of no return.

"Bea had prepared all these frozen casseroles, and with refrigeration gone we had to throw them out. We couldn't light the stove manually because of a safety sensor on the propane tank that's twelve-volt operated, and it just shut down.

"I called Mike Casinelli on KMI a high seas, American radio-communication station just before we lost all our power. I told him our last position and that he wouldn't hear from us again until we got to Hawaii.

"He said to get the sextant out and begin getting the navigational information ourselves.

"Well, I was really upset with myself at that point. I began to think, what the hell was I doing out here in the middle of the Pacific Ocean. We hadn't seen a boat since we left, and we didn't see another one until we got to Hawaii.

"I'm thinking, 'I've got my five kids and Bea, and I'm totally lost. I have no idea what the hell I'm doing. I couldn't sleep. I bet I didn't sleep two hours a day for the next ten days. I remember standing on the bow of the boat at night, crying, when I thought everyone else was asleep. It wasn't until years later my son Joe told me he could hear me crying from his bunk every night.

"Well, sure enough, Maria got that sextant out and, when the sun was shining, she would try to fix our position. Then, at night, she would take a star setting. We would do three of those a day and average them out on the little Japanese calculator that, along with the sextant, I didn't want to bring.

"Now she's getting good at it, and we're taking two fixes a day. The other children would say, 'Where are we, Dad?' I'd point down at a spot on the chart and say, 'We're right here.' I didn't know where the hell we were. I had no idea, but I didn't want to scare the kids.

"We couldn't even see the compass at night, but Joe had brought some glow sticks that you break and they stay lit for hours. Those were invaluable to us. I'd duct tape them to the compass and tell the kids to dead reckon as best they could at around 230 degrees on the compass. We had no idea how fast we were going, or how far off course we might have been—except for Maria's efforts on the sextant."

* * *

[Log Entry: We just had a little excitement. The fishing pole went berserk. We thought we had our first catch. After about a five-minute fight to get the fish in, it turned out to be a rag I had thrown overboard about five minutes earlier. I guess God meant for us to keep those dirty rags.]

The Virgilios would catch three more rags and a garbage bag before an actual fish was caught.

No refrigeration meant having to rely on the sea for dinner each night.

"So, we had to throw out our frozen food because we had no way to cook it. Bea rationed what we had, and we drank a lot of warm beer and soda and cold soup. It seemed the days were staying light longer. With little or no wind, we practically sat dead in the water. So much so, that we often had an hour swim around the boat for the kids.

"We had brought lots of our favorite music on cassettes but, again,

Navigator Maria and timer Joe.

we had nothing we could play them on. We couldn't take fresh water showers so we bathed in saltwater."

* * *

[Log Entry: . . . I must admit, at times I'm finding it difficult to be captain, engineer, deckhand, father, husband, dishwasher and doctor all at the same time. What this trip was billed as was "an adventure and challenge." So be it.]

"After nine days, and trolling with two fishing poles with nary a nibble, all of a sudden it was like God was looking down and saying, 'Virgilio, you idiot, you really got yourself into a bind here so I'm at least going to give you some food.'

"Every night, about five in the evening, these reels would start spinning, and we would land these huge mahi mahi and dorado. We were catching two a night. Joe got really good at fileting them, and Bea had brought a bunch of limes and would make ceviche out of the fish. That was a big hit, and it did wonders for our morale.

"I had brought a charcoal hibachi, but we had no propane. I did

Fisherman Joe became a very appreciated crewmember after we lost power.

have lighter fluid, so I would pour lighter fluid or gas from the outboard engine supply on to the charcoal and light it. Joe could then barbecue the fresh fish. We had grilled fish at night and ceviche during the day. We did that for seven days and seven nights. It was good. At least we wouldn't starve at sea.

"The kids would divvy up treats 'Four Oreo cookies for you, two Fig Newton's for me.' I'd hear them say, 'Okay, here's the deal. I'll give you two of my Oreos if you'll take fifteen minutes of my watch. Just wake me up fifteen minutes later.' They bartered the whole way to Hawaii.

* * *

"I suppose pulling watch wasn't the most fun for them. There were seven of us, so, in order to dog the watch, we did two, six-hour watches during the day, and three, four-hour watches at night. That way you weren't on the same watch every time.

"Bea and I started out taking the night watch, but then we all

Christiana working the foredeck.

began to rotate in and out. Gina didn't stand a watch, but was busy being the boat's gofer.

"It might be Joe and Maria on one watch, and Christiana and Angela on the next, and Bea and I on the third. And then Gina would float around as needed.

"Little Gina became quite good at the helm, and she was the master at finding things on the boat, which gave her an invaluable place on the crew, despite her young age and small size."

Bravo was a Kelly Peterson 46, center cockpit cutter. In the main cabin she had a port and starboard bunk. The table dropped down and made into a large bunk. There were two smaller bunks in the forepeak and there was a larger, master sleeping area aft. A rather large boat, she had 6'4" of headroom and could sleep seven.

At any given time, depending on the weather, two people were on watch and the other five would be down below. The forepeak, however, was unlivable when seas were rough.

Everyone hot bunked with the crew on watch—a navy term

Christiana, Angela and Joe bringing in a second fish.

applying to the assigning of more than one crewmember to a bed, to reduce sleeping space.

Bravo was an offshore cruising yacht. She drew six and a half feet of water, and flew a main, large jib, and a staysail. However, up forward, Bravo flew a loose-footed gennaker, which is larger than a jib but smaller than a spinnaker. On a mostly downwind sail, like the Hawaii voyage, the oversized headsail was an invaluable part of the Virgilio sail inventory.

* * *

[Log Entry: We are truly on our own and I must admit that the kids and Bea are handling it quite well. I know they are a little scared and concerned, but they are not sharing this with each other. Rather, they are sharing an up-beat mood. I am looking forward to my 9-midnight watch with Bea, so that I can hold her and feel the warmth of her love.]

"Christiana was my foredeck person. She knew how to handle sails better than anybody else, and I trusted her up there with me because we got so many sail wraps and tangles due to the fluky winds we encountered at times. Today Christiana is one of the most successful and groundbreaking woman skippers in the world of high-end, privately owned megayachts.

"My kids, God bless them."

"When the wind was positioned just right off our stern, we would try to fly wing and wing—with the main out to starboard and the genoa out to port—balanced by the spinnaker pole. It's tricky in the best of conditions because if you hit a gust or a bump, the spinnaker pole collapses, the main swings violently around, and everything gets tangled. It's a real mess.

"But my kids, God bless them, they all learned to sail pretty well. Of course, they spent a lot of time at the helm, and rarely did I have to come up from below and adjust their headings.

"Every day I'd dutifully go down and try to hand crank the generator but nothing would happen. And every night I would go up on the bow and literally pray and cry. I cried because I really felt like I had put my family in harm's way by being so totally incompetent at what I was doing, and not being fully prepared.

"I mean, you know, it was like going to do an operation with blinders on. I used to say that if it doesn't bleed, I can't fix it. Well, I certainly proved that on this trip. I just had no idea, number one, how far 2,300 miles of open ocean was. It's not like going to Catalina.

"As I said, there's nothing on your right side for as far as the eye can see, or your left. The solitude was intense. There was nothing in front of us we could see, or behind us. There was no place to stop. No way to communicate with anybody.

"We had a hand-held radio that had batteries that were somewhat charged, but I kept it off because there was no reason to use it, not that anyone could hear us anyway, and I figured we might need it when and if we got close to Hawaii, and then I could use it to call for assistance."

Dick and Maria calculating the noon position.

[Log Entry: Earlier today I got a little upset when the kids were fighting about something, but Maria put things in perspective when she said, "Dad, how can you expect us not to fight a little bit? And besides, what other children would even go on a week's vacation with their parents at our age?" She has a good point.]

"About that time I thought that I was being pretty clever, that the kids would never know how depressed and afraid I was about the whole thing.

"Every day, after we calculated our position, I would plot it on the table and the kids would gather around to see where we were on the chart.

"God bless, Bea, because the children never saw me break down. In front of them I was always very positive. I'd boldly point at the chart and say, 'We're right here. We've only got 1,800 miles to go, or whatever it was. My glass was half empty, but I sure didn't want them to know that.

"It had to be a little disappointing for them, because the chart was scaled to look at thousands of miles, and we were averaging maybe

120 miles a day. Therefore, the pencil mark depicting our position didn't move very far. If the children were depressed, or disheartened, they never let on in front of me.

"Meanwhile, the solitude of being alone on that big ocean, at night, and with all the worries constantly running through my mind, I just broke up. There is no way of explaining how devastated I felt, and how stupid I thought I was. At least I was able to hide that fear from the kids, or so I thought.

"Years later, when Joe wrote a college essay, his opening line was, 'I'm in the middle of the Pacific Ocean, and my father is on the bow, crying his eyes out.'

"I guess all the kids must have known. They never let on. Never let me know. I suppose it would be interesting one day to sit down with them and see what they all felt."

[Log Entry: At times I feel that I am being punished for something that I have done—some little indiscretion or whatever. For the life of me I cannot comprehend what awful thing I could have done to deserve what has happened to me this last several days.]

"Meanwhile, Maria continued to take sun sightings, and we plodded on, and on, and on. Finally, on her last fix, she put us maybe 100 or 150 miles off the coast of the big island of Hawaii.

"I wanted to go to Hilo because I didn't want to sail through the channel between Maui and the Big Island. It's very treacherous. So I went down and pulled out the coastal charts, which were larger and more detailed.

"It started to rain, and we hit squall after squall. According to Maria's last fix, we had to turn left thirty degrees. Still, I'm thinking I'm further south, and that if we do that we'll miss the whole state of Hawaii. I didn't want to commit to that dramatic of a course change until I could see some mass of land.

"Shit, what have I done?"

"If I could just see an island, any island, I'd feel better about

Maria getting a sun shot with Christiana timing.

making such a directional change. But low clouds obscured anything we might normally have been able to see.

"I'm sitting around procrastinating this decision. The kids are on watch, and finally they said to me, 'Dad, you always tell us that there's only one thing worse than a bad decision, and that's no decision. Do you want us to turn left or not?'

"Well, they were right, you know? I did always say that, and I still do. So, in my most authoritarian voice I said, 'Yeah, turn left thirty degrees right now.' Meanwhile I'm thinking to myself, 'Shit, what have I done?'

"All day long we saw nothing, even though I know there's a 13,000-foot volcano on the big island of Hawaii, so it's not like we're looking for Coronado, for God's sake.

"It's still raining and visibility is bad. Bea and I were up forward and, let me just say it again and again, God bless my wife. She never once said, 'You dumb shit, what have you done?' Not like the first Catalina trip, ha ha ha.

"That's what I was waiting for. I certainly deserved to have her call me out for being such an idiot. But she was very supportive. She knew I was hurting, and she just went about her business making sure the kids had what they needed. She'd make some crazy stuff out of canned food that we had been hoarding in case of emergency, even though we didn't need it. You know, we had fish all the time, and food-wise we were okay.

"I started bawling like a baby. I thought we were done for. What have I done to my family?"

"So, we had sailed all day, but still had not seen the island. It had been almost eight hours since we had made the thirty-degree course change to port. By then I was certain we had missed the whole state of Hawaii.

"Bea and I are up forward in the cabin. It was dark, and I forget who was on watch, but I said, 'Bea, you don't know what I've just done. I have no idea where we are. We just turned left thirty degrees, and we could miss the whole freaking state of Hawaii.'

"I said, 'We're out of provisions; we can't communicate with anybody.' And then I started bawling like a baby. I thought we were done for. What have I done to my family?

"I was severely chastising myself, praying to God to help us out, and I remember, in my prayers, I said, 'Dear God, if you get us out of

Everyone, even the navigator, had to steer.

here, I'll never make some stupid-ass mistake like this again, I'll never put my family in harm's way again, ever. Amen.' "

* * *

[Log Entry: Oh God, how I wish and pray that the children do not have bad memories of this trip.]

All of a sudden the kids started screaming like crazy. Bea and I put our heads out the hatch, and there, right off our bow were the brightest lights I'd ever seen. It was like driving into Nordstrom Fashion Valley at night, or flying an airplane out of the fog and seeing all the runway lights welcoming you.

"All I could mutter was, 'Holy shit!' There was Hilo, and right where Hilo was supposed to be — the only thing on that whole east coast of the big island. We were spot on and the kids were going nuts, jumping up and down, and hugging each other. Maria's navigational skills were being hailed as complete genius, which they were.

"Bea and I meanwhile just looked at each other. We knew who to thank and we muttered the words, 'God, thank you, God. You did this. Thank you, God.'

"On deck, everyone began running around and getting ready as though we were going to be there any minute. But it was night, and distance is deceiving at night, at sea. The lights are brighter because everything around them is total pitch-black darkness. But we still had twenty or thirty miles to go and the winds were light.

"As we got closer, I decided to use my hand-held radio to call the Coast Guard to just get some local knowledge. I turned it on and said, 'Coast Guard Hilo, Coast Guard Hilo. This is the sailing yacht Bravo.' When he answered back it was the best thing I had ever heard. I just beamed at that point. I had a total stranger on the other end of this radio, but he was my new best friend.

"He said, 'Sailing yacht Bravo, we've been expecting you. We've had a lot of calls from the mainland about you. Glad you made it.'

"I asked him for advice on the best way to get into the harbor. I explained I could see a couple of navigational lights and some physical landmarks. He quickly explained that a nighttime entrance would be foolish, very treacherous.

"He instructed us to heave to for the night. Hell, I had no idea what that meant, and confessed to him. He said to put our wheel all the way over, and our sail on the other side, to allow us to hold our position with the wind.

"Well, meanwhile the kids are all making plans to go to Chuck E Cheese, and they're down below putting on makeup and getting dressed. Bea was washing her hair with the foot-pedal shower, and she was also getting fixed up for our big appearance.

"I could see on the charts there was a breakwater that ran all up and down Hilo Harbor. And then the wind died, so I probably could have just sailed in. But the Coast Guard insisted I wait until morning. I figured we had come this far. There was no point in risking putting the boat up on the rocks.

"So we stayed offshore all night long. There were these intense open-ocean swells rolling under us the entire night. Enormous swells. It was the most miserable night I've ever spent on a boat.

"In hindsight, we could've sailed in there at night without any problem, but, again, I had no running lights. We obeyed the Coast Guard instructions and hove to. Then, when the sun came up, we could see clearly the huge entrance to that harbor.

"By morning the wind had died down to nothing. It was flat all around us except for the swells running under us. We must have been only a quarter of a mile from the beach so I called the Coast Guard and said I was going to try to sail in.

"They insisted I sit and wait. They suggested I drop the anchor. No way I was going to drop three hundred feet of chain with no electric windlass to retrieve it. Then he explained they couldn't tow sailboats unless there was an emergency on board.

"Well, now I'm thinking I should invent an emergency just to get them out here. We had traveled one hell of a long distance and were ready for this to be over.

"Meanwhile, fishing boats are beginning to come out of the harbor and pass us. I got out my hand-held and tried to reach them. One fellow said not to worry because the wind would come up at three in the afternoon. Well, I sure wasn't going to wait here all day long.

"I positioned the entire family, me, Bea, and the five kids along the rail and told them to look sick and miserable—like they were about to die. They didn't have to do much acting.

"I told one of the passing fishermen that we had nothing to eat, everyone was ill, and we couldn't wait until the afternoon winds. He didn't answer me—just kept motoring past me. Then, when he got about one hundred yards past me, he came on the radio and asked for our boat length. Apparently, he was a member of the Coast Guard Auxiliary.

"We were forty-six feet and he was about thirty-something. But he said if I could get him a hundred feet of line, he would try to get us in. So we frantically ran around the boat tying together everything we could find—halyards and everything.

"It was touch and go for awhile as he towed us in. At times we couldn't even see him because of the large swells rolling under us.

Meanwhile, the line is wrapped around our mainmast and every time there is slack in the line it's followed by this tremendous jerking sensation.

"We made it into the inner harbor, and we're about a mile or more from the docks. I figure we can sail the rest of the distance, but the fisherman shortened the scope on the line and offered to tow us in all the way.

"At that point I had Bea gather up all the cash she could find—about $150. He got us very close to the docks where we dropped the hook. Then Joe got in our tender and towed us backward the short distance to the dock.

"I waved the fisherman over and tried to give him the money. He wouldn't have anything to do with it. He gave us a big smile and a wave, and said, 'Welcome to Hilo.'

"After that, we wasted little time getting a hotel room with a swimming pool and buying ice cream—lots of ice cream. That night, when we all got into our beds, we were struck with a severe case of land sickness. We had our sea legs, but it took us awhile to get back our land legs."

The first thing Dick did was to bring a mechanic down to the boat. He had all the batteries replaced and repaired the impeller. Then, in true "belt & suspenders" fashion, he bought extra batteries.

After four or five days of rest and recovery in Hilo, the Virgilios loaded onto Bravo again and sailed to the other side of the island—the Kona Coast—where their vacation really began.

* * *

To say Dick dodged a bullet on that sailing trip would be an understatement. When asked what the smartest thing he brought was, he quickly answered, "the sextant."

When asked what the dumbest thing he brought was, he paused, and then let out a hearty laugh. "Myself!"

[Log Entry: July 15. As I look up at the stars and listen to the soothing music

of Christopher Cross, it is hard for me to believe that I am on my boat, anchored off Lahaina, some 2,300 miles from San Diego. I still cannot believe that we have completed the passage from San Diego. The entire trip seems like it happened in some foggy dream.

It wouldn't take much to coax me into keeping going—never going back to the rat race of trauma and vascular surgery, Mercy Hospital, tax shelters, accountants and lawyers.

Unfortunately, I have more than myself to think about and with five children yet to finish college, I guess the rat race is the only way for me to fulfill my responsibilities as a parent.

I just pray to God that someday Bea and I will have the opportunity to share moments like this alone, knowing that our family is grown and healthy, safe and happy.

Well, enough of this philosophizing. It's off to bed so that I can get up early and get Bravo on her way to Molokini. Good night.]

SIXTEEN

Midlife Crisis

Like every dream, the morning comes, the sun rises, and we are faced with the reality of day-to-day life. "Back to work!" So it was for Dick and his family after the Hawaii voyage.

They had been gone nearly six weeks. Despite a few unexpected circumstances, they survived the passage from San Diego to Hilo, and his heart, for the moment at least, felt strong and, if nothing else, still under warranty.

After such an adventure there wasn't much they felt they couldn't do. Extending their trip to sail around the Hawaiian Islands found them brimming with confidence, in both their boat and in their abilities to deal with the sea and all that came with such an adventure.

"We cruised all the state of Hawaii after making landfall in Hilo. We went around to the Kona Coast, over to Oahu, up to Kauai. We stopped in Maui and all the islands in between.

"When I got back home to San Diego, I couldn't help but reflect on that experience, both the good and the bad of it. I was amazed at how even the smallest detail came back to me from a particular smell, to the feeling of helplessness and fear at times, to our excitement at even the smallest victory aboard Bravo.

"Reflecting on that experience, I was, on one hand, really upset with myself for not being better prepared. Yet, on the other hand, I was so proud that I somehow managed to hold everything together—in spite of my having doubts about my ability to find the island and to get my family safely there.

"We returned to San Diego and put the kids back in school. After my first heart operation, I boldly declared I was going to change the priorities in my life. After the second operation I was never more certain that there were adventures in life I wanted to take, and adventures I wanted to share with my family.

I wanted to live, and even die if necessary, in the middle of a great adventure, with my wife and kids at my side.

"This meant I would take blocks of time off. Granted, I still worked a lot. And when I was at work, I worked long and hard. Then, after weeks and months of work, I would take a month off, usually in the summer when the kids were out of school, and we would go on a sailing adventure.

"In the winter, if I had a chance to take two or three weeks off, we would plan a skiing vacation. This was the new me. I had an entirely new bucket list and was determined not to waste my life away on the couch, a victim to my heart restraints. I wanted to live, and even die if necessary, in the middle of a great adventure, with my wife and kids at my side.

"I always believed there were a lot of guys out there who could do what I did medically, so I just convinced myself to let them do it, and, even though I was still a good doctor, and a hard-working one at that, this time around I began to make time with my family. It was a new era for Dick Virgilio; that much I was certain of.

"So now I'm back to work, but, it's not like the navy when you just go on vacation and continue to collect your paychecks. Now, if I didn't work, I didn't get paid. I either had to be working in trauma, building my vascular surgery practice, or helping Dr. Houseman with his heart operations."

In the back of Dick's mind he was eternally grateful for the second fix on his heart. Likewise, he was experiencing a great level of personal and professional fulfillment watching Mercy Hospital benefit from the new trauma center.

But he hadn't forgotten the promise to his family to keep them his chief priority. Doctors had told him earlier he most likely wouldn't live to see 55. Based on that, Dick had created his bucket list. While he had accomplished a few items on the list, there were some things he had yet to complete—running a marathon and sailing singlehanded to Hawaii were just the beginning.

Being at sea for seventeen days alone makes a marathon look like a cake walk.

"Actually, if I were completely honest, I had always wanted to do those two things. They didn't just appear on my new bucket list out of the blue. It wasn't until people started telling me what I couldn't do that I decided, hell, I'm going to run in a marathon. And I'm going to sail to Hawaii, alone.

"I was turning 50, and maybe I was having a midlife crisis. But for me, some could say it was an end-of-life crisis.

"These were both high mountains to climb, even for individuals with normal hearts. For me they should have been impossible. I would soon learn how difficult each would be to accomplish.

"The marathon would be over in a day. The solo boat race and having to deal with weather, sail changes, and the loneliness of being at sea, would take seventeen days, with each day being its own marathon. In retrospect, this made the marathon look like a cakewalk.

"Well, that's what I wanted to do. I made up my mind, and I flat refused to run out my days as an invalid on a couch. At that point, I was finally accomplishing my dreams of spending time with my family. I was teaching my kids, but I was also learning from them a lot. Still, deep down, I wanted to say I accomplished this singlehanded

Dick finishing the Marathon, December 1986.

race to Hawaii simply because it was something few other people have done."

Maybe Dick was just trying to prove something to Dick. There is nothing like heart surgery to remind you of your mortality. But in his case, there was also an adventurer lurking deep inside, impatient to come out.

"As far as running the marathon, hell, I didn't even train. Before that day, the furthest I had ever run was six miles. Unfazed, I signed up. My daughter Christiana was running in it as well, and I just decided I was gonna do this with her. No time like the present, and, truth be known, I really had no intention of finishing the damned thing."

And that's how it came to pass that Dick Virgilio, at age 50, and with a history of two heart attacks and two heart bypass operations began his first and last marathon.

The race started in Balboa Park near the San Diego Zoo. It wound its way down through the city and passed right by the San Diego Yacht Club.

"Yeah, I think we hit the ten-mile marker at the yacht club. All my friends were out on the street cheering, because I had told Bea that when we got to the yacht club, I was just going to turn left, jump into the Jacuzzi and relax. They were all there to celebrate my 'trying' to run a marathon.

"I initially thought I'd run a little bit of the way with my daughter, but she was far ahead of me from the very beginning. Then, as I approached the yacht club, I looked around at the group I was running with and thought, 'Shit, these guys aren't that much better than I am.'

"So I yelled over at Bea that I was going to keep going. I remember her yelling, 'No, no you don't want to go that far,' but I just yelled back that I was going to finish this thing if I could.

"Well, the yacht club quickly faded into the background. We headed up over Point Loma, down into Mission Beach, and all along the boardwalk over to Mission Bay Drive. We finished at Sea World.

"About mile twenty I was really, really hurting—my breathing was rough and my legs were gone. I wanted to stop but something inside told me that I couldn't quit. I kept telling myself there were just four more miles to go . . . just four more miles.

"Then, when I thought I couldn't run another step, a complete stranger sidled up next to me. He was one of the highly competitive walkers in the marathon. Ha-ha. That's how slow I was going. Even the walkers were beating me.

"Anyway, the guy he had been pacing and competing against pulled ahead and left him. He saw me and said, 'I know what you're feeling. I'll tell you what I'm going to do. I'll walk alongside while you run. I'm going to keep you going.' And, by God, he did.

"I never saw him again after that. Even though he was faster walking than I was running, he spent the entire last four miles right next to me, talking to me, encouraging me, telling me to take breaths, and warning me not to stop. I wish I could find that very kind walker to thank him again. What a great guy he was.

"And that's how I ran my one and only marathon—a medical disaster with no training whatsoever."

It would be just over a year until Dick would experience his third heart attack and third open heart surgery.

***

"This bucket list stuff was starting to get fun. I was doing things I had only dreamed of until then. And it seemed like after each heart operation I felt younger, stronger, and more eager to tackle the next thing on my list.

"I was always on the lookout for ways to promote and raise money for the Trauma Research and Education Foundation. I felt really strongly about that, obviously. We needed more research and greater education, even if it was just getting more kids to wear bike helmets.

"So I put together this concept we called 'Race For Life.' I arranged to have an identical boat to mine donated for the race, a Kelly Peterson 46, which is an extremely reliable blue-water cruising design. The plan was for two of us, one man on each boat, to race from San Diego to Hawaii.

"The natural selection for such an unusual competition seemed to be Sandy Purdon, a good friend, and a popular and successful sailor at San Diego Yacht Club.

"We solicited a bunch of sponsors. The news media discovered us, and they began to do a lot of our work for us—promoting the race in the newspapers and on TV, and attracting more interest from the community at large, which in the end raised more money for our cause.

Bravo *and* Spirit *in San Diego Bay at the start of the single-handed Race For Life to Hawaii.*

"By the time we left the dock, we had managed to raise $170,000 and more was coming in. People were beginning to understand what Trauma was, and to understand that it was a disease that had to be dealt with.

"Well, the closer we got to the actual race, the more committed I became. But I also grew more scared. I mean, it probably wasn't the smartest thing for me to do, to schedule a singlehanded race across the Pacific Ocean, what with my heart condition and all. I was fifty years old, after all.

"But this was something I really wanted to prove that I could do. If I were successful, it would put those fears behind me, for good.

"I think it was John Wayne who said, 'Courage is being scared to death and saddling up anyway.' Based on that, I suppose you could say I had great courage, but was severely lacking in the intelligence department prior to that solo sail across the Pacific. All I know is that I was scared shitless as the time grew nearer."

Leading up to his departure, there were numerous events designed to celebrate the Race For Life and the two men who picked up the gauntlet of battle. There were fundraising dinners, parties, a luau here and there, and lots of TV interviews.

"On the day of our departure, my entire family was there to cheer me on. Even though my father and brother had been distant for a very long time, they both turned out. Maybe they thought I was going to disappear mid-ocean and this was their way of paying their respects.

"Whatever the reason, I had done my homework for the voyage. I had provisioned smartly, I thought. And, after all, I had done this crossing before and had a pretty good idea of what to expect between San Diego and Hawaii.

"Still, as I passed Point Loma to starboard I had the loneliest feeling in my gut. Of course, winds were right out of the south that morning, so it took us forever just to beat out of the channel and San Diego Bay.

Virgilio, you dumb shit.
What have you done?

"Here we are in overstocked, identical, 46-foot cruising boats that don't go to weather very well even in the best of conditions. Before we reached the ocean we found ourselves in a tacking duel just to get clear of Point Loma. We were barely able to sail forty degrees off the wind.

"I think we did more tacks just getting out of San Diego Bay than we did the rest of voyage. And all around us was this huge flotilla of boats—family and friends, all helping send us on our way, with horns blasting continuously in support.

"It was overcast and the seas were rough outside the harbor. I remember looking behind me from the helm and seeing them all turn back for home.

"I had spent my life doing all these things to create a better world for my family. I began to reflect on all the surgeries I had undergone to get healthy, for them. Then it dawned on me, 'Virgilio, you dumb shit. What have you done?'"

***

When talking to Bea about conversations leading up to Dick's solo sail to Hawaii, she admits to telling him how crazy he was to do this, but try as she might, she couldn't talk him out of it. God knows she gave it her best, most impassioned shot, but Dick was stubborn, even more so than most men.

"He wanted to do this, and that's the way it was going to be," she said. "Absolutely I didn't want him to go. And when he would tell me things like, 'Don't worry, honey, you and the kids will be taken care of if anything happens to me,' I just looked at him and told him he was a complete lunatic.

"I suppose I get that way every time he goes to sea, even when he's sailing with our daughter on her big yacht. I'm generally okay the first day, but the second day brings lots of worry and thoughts about 'what if.'

"Richard was making regular updates on-air at a San Diego radio station, the Hudson and Bauer Show," Bea said. "I remember how heartening it was to hear his voice, even though I could tell he was half asleep during most of those communications. I could hear the fatigue in his voice, and that was hard for me to listen to.

"I have to tell you a funny story that took place at the race start. As we were following him out of the Gulch from the yacht club, he ran his boat aground in front of our house. Of course, he won't admit to that today," said Bea, laughing.

Sort of like the three-second rule when you drop a piece of food, if you pick it up quickly, it's as if it never happened. Fortunately, Dick was able to work his way off the sand quickly and resume his departure, but the brief grounding was just the beginning of his problems.

"Once we left the calm of the channel, the seasickness kicked in, as is par for the course on a voyage like this, or at least for me. I can tell you now that I wondered at that moment if the last sight of my family would be in the distance, sailing away from me, barely recognizable on the horizon, as little arms waved continually.

"So there we were, finally alone at sea. Sandy and I were trying to sail the correct heading to put us on a rhumb line to Hawaii from this latitude. The bow of the boat was crashing into waves, sliding down the other side, and making this tremendous jerking motion as the sails reset to the wind.

"I was lying on my belly in the cockpit throwing up. I was cold and wet because water was coming over the bow and washing back to the cockpit. You don't even want to know my thoughts at that moment, but I can tell you I was having doubts about this latest adventure. Serious doubts.

"Sandy Purdon is a very competitive and accomplished sailor. Of course, my innocent impression of this whole race was that we would sail in tandem to Hawaii, or at least within sight of one another, so if one of us got in trouble, the other guy would be there.

"Sandy didn't waste any time in getting into racing mode. I awoke the next morning and scanned the horizon. No Sandy. Winds were blowing twenty to twenty-five knots out of the northwest and my halyards were banging like crazy as this large beam sea kept crashing into my boat.

"Sandy, I soon discovered, headed south under cover of darkness. His strategy was to seek better sailing conditions down there. Before the race, Sandy had consulted with Dan Brown, a big weather guru at the yacht club.

"Here's a guy who forecasted TransPac races. I often wonder if Sandy actually hired Dan or not. I guess I was just jealous that I hadn't thought to do it myself. All I know is they spent a lot of time together prior to the race, and suddenly the competition had disappeared off my radar. I couldn't even hail Sandy on my VHF radio.

"Sandy was gambling on the trades filling in early, and at a latitude much further south than the rhumb line to Hawaii. But in his search for better air, we must have been 300 miles apart. It was apparent that one of us was going to win big. Which one, neither of us could be sure.

"I finally reached him on the single-sideband radio. 'Where are you?' I asked. He said he wasn't going to tell me. 'This is a race,' he shot back over the radio.

"I got really angry. I mean, I was pissed, and I felt a little betrayed at that point. I always knew he was a better sailor—his trophy shelf was much larger than mine, and his sailing resume far more impressive. I get it that yacht club pride was also at stake, and that probably meant a lot more to him than to me.

"I was just an old doctor, saddled with medical issues, who wanted to raise money for my charity—trauma care. I didn't know shit about the tactics involved in racing twenty-three hundred miles to Hawaii.

"So, here I was, a grown man, alone on his little boat, in the middle of the sea, and I was steaming with anger. It never occurred to me this would be a boxing match where your opponent threw punches at you from below the horizon.

"Well, in a few days the trade winds filled in and fortunately for me, from the north, which gave me a temporary lead. My attitude improved vastly, and I got down to the business of sailing my boat.

"The sun came out and it got warmer. I got used to the motion as the beam seas disappeared and were on my stern quarter.

"At that point I wasn't thinking strategies, course tactics, or secret weapons. I knew the only thing I could do was to sail as tight a boat as I knew how, and make as few mistakes as possible.

"One advantage I had over him was that, as a surgeon, throughout my whole life I was used to getting up every two or three hours. In Vietnam, that was the norm. Even now I never sleep through until morning. I'm perpetually waiting for that phone to ring in the middle of the night. Old habits are hard to break."

After his sailing experience to Hawaii with the family, Dick had learned some lessons the hard way. On this voyage he carried two autopilots. One was a wind-driven autopilot and the other an electric one. He didn't want to get caught with his pants down again, so he subscribed to the "belt & suspenders theory" of provisioning for this voyage.

"If I didn't make it this time, it wouldn't be because of mechanical failure. It would be because of human failure."

Still, nothing could have prepared him for a factor he hadn't considered.

***

"I was incredibly lonely. The sensory deprivation was killing me. You have no input from anybody, anywhere. I began to talk to the voices—the vibration of the wind and rain in the rigging. It was actually like someone was talking back to me out there. After a week or so, I began to think somebody was actually on the boat with me. I began to hallucinate.

"One night I found myself on my hands and knees with a flare gun, trying to find the little shit who was talking to me non-stop. The more I read about it when I got back, the more I realized that wasn't so unusual for guys who sail singlehandedly. They all hear voices generated from wind and vibrations in the rigging.

"Eventually, I began to talk to myself and say things like, 'Look, you're an educated doctor for God's sake. You know there's nobody else on this boat, so why are you going there?' But it was very real to me, and sometimes it was more than one person talking to me. It was extremely vivid, and, oddly enough, we had some great conversations at times.

"At one point I contacted Sandy on the radio and told him about it. I said, 'Sandy, I'm losing it. We've been out here eight or nine days and I swear to God these guys are on my boat and talking me to death.'

"Sandy says, 'Well, thank God they're over there. They were here last night.'

What an insignificant little creature I am.

"After that I felt a lot better, just knowing I wasn't the only insane person floating around out there. The biggest contribution to keeping my sanity was a photo of Bea and the kids that I kept on the bulkhead where I could see it all the time. Believe me when I tell you I sought refuge in that photo, a lot."

[LOG ENTRY: This evening is rather pleasant. The clouds have broken a little bit. The wind is blowing 7–10 knots. I am on a beam reach going about 5–6 knots with the self-steering vane piloting the boat. I'm listening to a Diana Ross tape and having a glass of wine with some cheese and crackers.]

"Every day, as the sun went down and darkness enveloped everything around me, I became uneasy. You get so disoriented at night. Everything turns black and you can't see the ocean. I was always glad to see the sun come up at dawn.

"As I looked out at miles and miles and miles of ocean and cloudy skies, it made me realize what an insignificant little creature I am in this vast, vast ocean. I had not seen another light, another boat, or anything since my first night at sea. That was the last time I saw Sandy."

[LOG ENTRY: I am thinking about the people in my life who have meant so much to me through the years. Thinking how much I love Bea and my kids, and wondering if I have been a good father and a good husband. Lord knows I have tried. But you never know. At times I have been sort of an ass, like everybody else. I just hope the people that I love understand how hard I try to be a good person.]

"One thing I found was that the autopilots weren't as accurate as my own two hands on the helm. Frequently I would awake in the middle of the night and turn them off. I'd manually steer the boat for three or four hours straight. Then I'd put it back on automatic when I had to go forward to change a sail or do something on the bow.

"For example, we had a racing/safety rule-of-thumb that we would take our gennaker down every night. Of course, when darkness came upon us that was usually when the winds picked up.

"Dousing the gennaker was a real chore. We had these bags that we would pull down to stuff the gennaker into. So, we pull the sock down and end up with the stupid thing wrapped up all around us like a damned cocoon.

"Every time I'd get the sail half way down, there would be a little wind shift and it would fill with wind and lift me right off the deck. If someone's on the helm, they can adjust for it. But, with the autopilot on, it's not quite such a smooth operation.

"I finally had enough of that. I devised a way to sit with my back against the mast. I'd flake the lines on the deck beside me and just let go of the halyard. The sail would go 'Whoomp' and straight out. Then I'd just pull it in, hand over hand. It wasn't pretty, but it worked.

"The trick was to get it on deck before the boat ran over it. Fortunately, I was able to accomplish this every time. They say it's better to be lucky than good. That definitely describes me.

"I don't mind admitting that those little daily exercises of dousing the gennaker scared the shit out of me. It got to where I thought I might have to have a drink before I attempted it, just to calm myself. Still, as good as I got at it, there was usually an hour where the boat was sailing under main alone before I managed to get the headsail out to run in a wing-and-wing configuration, and before I could finally return to the cockpit."

Taking the gennaker down was not the only time that Dick had to venture to the bow of the boat. Each time he had to turn, to gybe the boat going downwind, he had to douse whatever sail, jib or gennaker, switch the gennaker pole from one side to the other, then redeploy the appropriate headsail.

All this time on the bow, Dick was praying constantly that the mechanical autopilot did not accidently gybe the boat while he was in such a vulnerable position. Each time there was a sail change, Dick had to go through this maneuver, this dance. He was, by his own admission, scared to death that he would screw it up and possibly lose the rig or, worse, injure himself in the process.

During his daily dance with headsails, Dick wrestled with heavy aluminum poles (no carbon fiber on this voyage). All of this required an enormous amount of upper body strength. And while up there grappling with the gennaker, his thoughts were constantly worrying about what could go wrong.

"The boat is being steered mechanically. Mechanical things can and do break. What if one of these heavy poles strikes me in the head?"

He would later admit he didn't keep track of how many trips to the bow he had to make, but that he was certain of one thing: over the course of this long voyage, each trip to the bow was more traumatic than the one prior. And, as great as his fear was of going forward to douse the gennaker every night, or gybe the boat, his enthusiasm at getting back to the helm, to his little sanctuary at the rear of the boat, was far greater.

The entire time at sea, Dick was tethered to the boat by a lifeline. He lived in his life vest. If washed overboard, he might not be found, but he would stay afloat. The lifeline was his safety umbilical cord. If he had been washed overboard, he would have, in theory, remained attached to the boat. Whether Dick could have climbed back on board is another question, but in a situation like that, he could only plan as well as he could and hope for the best. Prayer is also a handy companion.

His log entry sums it up best:

[LOG ENTRY: . . . and I tell you, every night it takes me an hour or more to douse that gennaker. I feel like I have cheated death ten times. I am totally exhausted, my back hurts, my neck hurts, I want to cry . . .]

Years earlier, while serving in Vietnam, Dick learned a valuable lesson: "There is only one thing worse than a bad decision, and that's no decision." Throughout this voyage he agonized again and again over decisions about safety, navigation, and just about everything one could imagine. But, in the end, he knew deep down that only he could make the decision, and so it was. No one knew this better than Dick Virgilio.

***

[LOG ENTRY: I just hit 9 knots of boat speed. I'm listening to a Whitney Houston tape and had a little glass of wine. I see squalls all around me, and I just wonder what's going to happen when I have to go through one of those suckers. I am getting physically tired. I hope that I can make it to the end out here without making some stupid mistake just because of fatigue.]

"Finally, about day sixteen, I had been getting lifts that were carrying me away from the Hawaiian Islands. I realized that if I didn't gybe, I was going to end up in Japan.

[The] boat shook like it had been hit by a howitzer.

"Meanwhile, Sandy was on a nice point of sail, headed straight towards Diamondhead.

"In what was the biggest decision of the trip for me, I elected

to gybe the boat. It was about ten p.m., dark as hell, and I was in the middle of a rainsquall. I knew it was either make this maneuver or kiss the race goodbye. Even today, Sandy tells the story that he never thought I would gybe my boat that night, what with all the crazy wind and rain I was experiencing. But I had to do it.

"I remember saying to myself out loud that night,

The marathon lasted only several hours; the Race For Life lasted 17 days. Dick's exhaustion after two weeks at sea is captured in this photo taken from video feed near the end of the race.

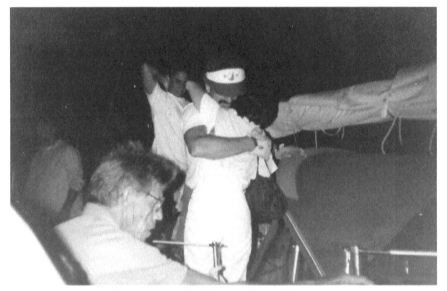

Bea welcoming Dick the night he finished the race.

'Self? If you're ever going to have another heart attack, it's gonna happen during this gybe.' That's how big a decision this was. That's how scared I was before committing to that course of action.

"Even though I sheeted in the mainsail and genoa, once I gybed the entire boat shook like it had been hit by a howitzer. I thought I was gonna rip the mast right out of the boat. But at that point Sandy was leading the race. Had I not gybed, I would never have been able to make the finish line the next day. As it was, I gybed and, finding myself on a favorable point of sail, I quickly regained the lead."

The following day Dick's decision to gybe was rewarded big time. After 17 days, many of those averaging 150 miles a day, he beat Sandy to the finish line by 12 hours and nearly 70 miles. Ironically, Dick's first Hawaii trip with the family was fraught with breakdowns and mistakes. This trip was sailed more machine-like, with a focus on safety and not making errors. Still, Dick had finished the race in the same amount of time it took him and his family to make the trip on this same boat — 17 days.

"This singlehanded trip made a marathon look like a cakewalk. I

Dick and Bea's reunion in Hawaii.

was mentally and physically destroyed from this voyage. The nightly sail changes, the worrying, and then, just when you think you've got everything under control, you hear yourself screaming from the fore-deck to an invisible person at the helm, 'Steer the boat up, steer it up, damn it.' And, of course, there's nobody in the cockpit.

"And then you get on your knees and look back aft. There's still forty feet you've got to crawl to get back to the cockpit. But somehow you do it; you get to the cockpit and make the helm adjustment, then crawl back to the bow to finish what you started."

The sail to Hawaii was filled with the unexpected. Dick had radar but he said it beeped every five minutes and he couldn't sleep, so he just never used it.

Once, about two days from Hawaii, he was at the helm in the

Sandy and Kathy Purdon together with Dick and Bea at finish of Race For Life.

middle of the night. All of a sudden these lights came on and a sub-marine surfaced off the starboard quarter. It was a Russian submarine.

Then, with the finish so close he could taste it, all he had to do was cross the Molokai Channel. As he did, the wind had gone to the other side of his boat, filled the main and pushed the boat off course just enough for his jib boom to cross over. He had been hit by an unex-pected gust, and it forced a gybe. As his gennaker flapped, the boom swung violently to the other side of the boat. Fortunately, it rode high and didn't take Dick's head off.

In a later retelling of the experience, he agreed it was the ultimate bitch slap, and he still shudders remembering that feeling of helpless-ness, watching as his boat sailed to the edge of breakage.

✳✳✳

"That Molokai crossing was crazy. It's a rough crossing, what with the wind and the cross surf that comes in. I could see Diamondhead maybe thirty or forty miles in the distance, but I didn't finish until midnight.

"There was no finish line per se; no buoy I had to sail around or past. The rules stated you just had to cross this imaginary line within four miles of Diamondhead. I had survived the unintentional gybe but the big genoa was wrung out on a pole. I was sailing under main only, and I was steering myself, without the benefit of autopilot.

"After that surprise gybe, I was plenty scared. There was no way I was going to trust my life to that autopilot in those conditions. So there I was, at the helm, darkness setting in, and I have to pee. The hell with it, I thought. I just peed right there in the cockpit.

"I needed to report in but there was no way I was leaving the helm to go below. So I fired up the handheld. The race committee sent a boat out to officially log my finish and that was a bit of an effort, too, as I had to signal them my whereabouts in the dark. It was not an easy finish. Finally, over the radio, they said, 'Okay, Bravo, we see you. You have officially crossed the finish line. Congratulations on your win.'

"No time to celebrate. The wind continued to blow like stink, and I still had to roll that big genoa in and get the pole down. I also had to lower the main. Suddenly I heard this motor. I looked over and saw a rigid-hulled inflatable coming in close. They were yelling that they were here to help me. Before I knew it, three of them had come on board.

"I guess their celebration started a bit earlier, because they were all three drunk. But everything worked out. Coming into the Hawaii Yacht Club, I could hear the guy with the deep voice announcing the boat's name and my name over the intercom, describing how our efforts would help advance trauma care.

"It's funny now to think about it, but as I was coming in to the dock that night, my family was all there waiting for me. I yelled at my son Joe to prepare to catch a line as I headed in towards the dock. The three drunken crewmembers I had suddenly inherited just stood there. I yelled for them to heave the line, but they didn't have a clue what I was talking about. So, after doing this crazy trans-Pacific crossing alone, I had to do an extremely humiliating go-around at the dock before I could come in.

"Boy, what a feeling. I mean, once I passed Diamondhead, I was hit with the sobering reality of what I had just done. I was so proud of myself. I didn't break the boat; I didn't have a heart attack; and I lived to tell the story. And the best part was that we raised some money for trauma care, and I beat San Diego Yacht Club's fair-haired boy.

"The irony of the finish was that I finished in the dark, with little fanfare and three drunken crewmembers on board. Sandy finished 12 hours later, in daylight, with helicopters overhead and boats of photographers. Unfortunately, the only photos of our two boats together were what were taken before we departed San Diego—staged shots. On this day I was a spectator, on a committee boat, watching Sandy cross the finish line.

"But, you know, if you asked me to describe to you the greatest physical accomplishment of my life, that crossing was the real deal. It wasn't my football years or playing lacrosse or wrestling. It wasn't the marathon. This adventure tested me and pushed me on every level—physically, mentally, and spiritually. There were times when I was so physically and mentally exhausted, and scared 24/7, I didn't know if I would live to see the next day. But I did.

***

"I prayed a lot on this trip. Mostly I prayed that I would see my kids and Bea again. I really was hard on myself, constantly calling myself a 'dumb shit' for doing this. Unless you've gone through such a horrendous challenge as a singlehanded voyage, you can't really understand what goes through a man's mind. Shit, the first night of the race I actually considered turning around and going back home. I had been throwing up all night and was in a very weakened condition.

"But, once you're out there, you begin to realize you CAN do this, and you begin to focus on the things you have to do to stay alive and keep the boat moving forward. You've got to navigate, you've got to cook, and you've got to eat. In my case I also had to communicate with Hudson & Bauer, the radio talk show hosts (and the ghosts on board). But, you know what? As tired as I was, that was something I looked forward to.

"I suppose about five days out I realized I had passed the point of no return. At that point I stopped thinking about quitting and began to think about winning. I was no longer obsessing about what I perceived to be a betrayal on Sandy's part when he sailed away from me. In fact, I had to help him over the radio at one point. His bilge pump wasn't working. Since I knew the Peterson better (he was on a borrowed boat), I was able to walk him through a repair over the radio.

"You know, as I sat out there floating around on Bravo, all alone, I had a lot of time to think. One of the things that kept coming back to me was when I ran away from home at thirteen and hitchhiked across the country, alone.

"I remembered how scared I was during that little adventure. And yet, I was absolutely determined not to turn around and go back. I continually reminded myself of that as I fought to keep moving forward in that singlehanded race to Hawaii—fighting my fears and weaknesses every watery mile of the way.

"Yes, I was scared. I was petrified. And yet, something inside of me kept me going across that ocean at age fifty. Because of my heart condition then, I was no better equipped than that thirteen-year-old kid hitchhiking across the country.

"I wasn't running away from anything on the boat trip. But I was breaking down barriers and seeking new horizons, just as I did as a kid standing there on a dark road, alone, with my thumb out, and no idea where in the hell I was."

Once in Hawaii, Dick began to recover quickly. Having his family with him was the best medicine a person could ever hope for. They were kept busy with interviews. Dick met the mayor of Honolulu and presented him a gift from San Diego's mayor. There were proclamations, awards, and plaques, and a multitude of accolades, and it never seemed to end. When they got back to San Diego, the awards and honors started up all over again.

"Bea and the kids seemed to get a kick out of all the attention I was receiving. Or, maybe they were just glad I was still alive. And, yes, I was very proud that I had beaten Sandy, especially after his racing tactic our first night at sea. You know what Sandy? It WAS a race. And I won."

POSTSCRIPT: Sandy, I would like you to know how much I appreciate your willingness to participate in this crazy adventure, and your help in raising money for the Trauma Research and Education Foundation. You are a true friend. And we had quite an adventure—you, me . . . and the ghosts. Didn't we?

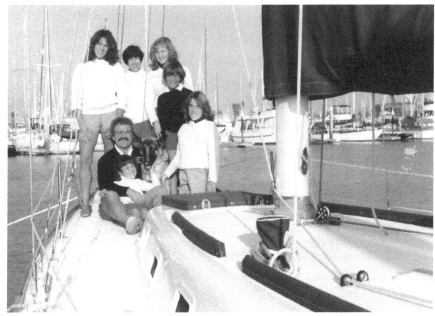

The family on the foredeck of their Cal 40, 1979.

Like father, like son. Unlike Dick and his father, Joe loved to emulate his Dad.

SEVENTEEN

"Interesting Decade"

Dick and his family experienced a mixture of adventures on and off the water in the decade following the Race For Life in 1987. Among those "adventures" were continued heart problems resulting in a third heart bypass operation.

There were sailing voyages extending from Glacier Bay, Alaska, to Manzanillo, Mexico, and there were four more Hawaii trips on Bravo and Swiftsure, with various combinations of his children. Dick also found time for a trans-Atlantic crossing with his daughter Christiana, and a much-anticipated sail to Tahiti with his son Joe.

As this was happening, he was rewarded with one of the highest compliments from his peers at the San Diego Yacht Club. He was elected to the board of directors and slated to become commodore in 1997.

With five children to put through college during these years, he couldn't retire from his real job, although he desperately wanted this to happen. Perhaps the greatest motivator for retirement was his ongoing heart problems.

His bucket list had Dick sailing his own boat to the South Pacific and cruising through the various island chains all the way to Australia. In spite of his health problems, he accomplished all of this before the close of the 20th century. This included finally retiring from medicine—a profession that he was rapidly becoming disenchanted with.

"I had a feeling that the stress of the singlehanded race would eventually have an adverse effect on me,—take its toll on me—but even I was surprised at how quickly I began to go downhill after my return to San Diego. Within six months I found myself facing yet another major and life-altering decision."

Dick adjusted quickly to life ashore after the Race For Life. He had lost some weight on the voyage but quickly put it back on. Although he wrestled in high school at about 205 lbs., his ideal weight was about 185 lbs. The tough part was all the parties and events he had to attend upon returning from the Race For Life. Throughout his lifetime he had to watch his weight. If unchecked, he would go up like a balloon. Post-Race For Life, rich food and alcohol seemed to be the norm, not the exception.

"So the question loomed in front of me: should I have a third heart operation that, if successful, would allow me the opportunity to stay active? Or should I be relegated to an encumbering series of medications and become a couch potato?

"I knew better than anyone the risks of a third heart procedure, but the alternative was unacceptable. As might be expected, Bea and the children were not so sure about it, but I didn't want them seeing me as this house-bound invalid.

"The decision had to be mine, and I had to make the best decision I could, not just for me, but for my family. I also knew that I was far too athletic to succumb to meds and daytime TV. Look, I just would not make a good couch potato at all, and you can bet I would have been miserable to live with.

"So, despite the significant risk, once again my friend and partner Lee Housman operated on me, stopping my heart for a third time and fixing the problem.

"It was extremely comforting for me as I went under anesthesia to be surrounded by all those familiar faces that I had worked with in the operating room at Mercy. I knew I was in good hands and that all would turn out well. I also felt comfort in knowing that if things didn't turn out well, I had accomplished a lot in my short fifty-two years. For the first time I felt content my legacy would live on through my children.

"I tell everyone that I was not scared to have that third surgery, but to be honest, I was scared, really scared. I didn't believe, deep down, that I would survive.

"Boy, was I happy to wake up and have it over with. Now, as I look back over the years, I can't believe it's been nearly three decades since that operation. I have not had another significant heart attack during that time, although I have had five operations to place (and replace) internal defibrillators in my chest in an attempt to control ventricular fibrillation."

Defibrillator devices are small—maybe three inches round. They have wires going through the vein into the heart. They are designed to cure arrhythmia issues. A device is placed in the chest wall and senses the heart rhythm. When the heart rate becomes too fast to be effective, it shocks the heart. The theory being that by shocking and stopping the heart momentarily, it will then start back up with a normal rhythm.

Dick had definite opinions about the procedure and the after effects:

"If it works right, it hurts like hell, but it saves your life. The reality is, if you're standing up when it hits, it will knock you to the ground and a few feet to the side. But that's the price you pay."

"It's like having a tiny time bomb in your chest and never knowing when you're gonna get a shock that's strong enough to throw you across the room. The problem is that it doesn't always work as it's supposed to. If a wire is broken and you get a short in the mechanics of the device, it just keeps shocking your heart. You can imagine the danger in that, and the wear on the heart, no matter how strong it or you might be. If left untreated, it can result in death.

Skiing in Lake Tahoe, 1981.

"These devices have saved my life numerous times. Yet, due to faulty wiring, they have caused me to be shocked unnecessarily on several occasions, and for prolonged periods of time."

Dick's defibrillator device malfunctioned five times between 1996 (when the first one was put in) and 2012. During those 15 years, each of those incidents involved another chest operation.

"One time the wiring got screwed up while we were in Russia and I couldn't get it fixed there. Well, there was no way I was gonna die in Russia, so I decided to fly home with a defibrillator that now had a mind of its own. It would fire randomly, whether I needed to be shocked or not.

I still can't get myself to buy green bananas.

"It went off several times in St. Petersburg. Then it went off again in the Helsinki Airport before I could board a non-stop flight to New York. As if that wasn't enough torture, I was in JFK airport walking down a corridor to the gate, to board my flight home, and it went off again. This time I found myself across the hall, flat on the floor, with

Dick with family while cruising in British Columbia, 1984.

people stepping over me and saying things like, 'I hope they don't let this drunk on the plane.' So much for concern and compassion in our society.

"Bea was scared to death and wanted to call 911 and get me to a hospital in New York. But I wanted to get home so badly that I overruled her, and we boarded the flight to San Diego. Fortunately, I arrived without any further shocks or surprises. Upon landing, I immediately went to the hospital to get it fixed.

"Anyway, I had lived forty-three years knowing that I had a bad ticker since my first heart operation but I never let the fear of dying interfere with my activities. It's hard for me to believe that I have been able to live this long. I am so very grateful, thankful, and fortunate.

"Every morning I wake up and feel extremely Blessed to be alive. However, deep down, I know it could all come to a screeching halt in an instant, and, knowing that, I still can't get myself to buy green bananas.

***

"In 1986, the year before the Race for Life, my good friend George Folgner and I bought a seventy-foot downwind sled called Swiftsure. We purchased her from another close friend, Nick Frazee. I figured nobody was going to beat my door down to get me to crew in a Hawaii race on one of these seagoing racehorses. So I decided that if I was ever going to have that experience I would either have to charter or buy a boat.

"When the opportunity arose to purchase Swiftsure, I jumped at it. Of course, I needed another boat like I needed a hole in my head. And I'm sure Bea would vouch for that. But George and I had a plan to charter the boat for long distance downwind races, of which there were plenty.

"The way we figured it, our boat, because of its extensive racing pedigree, would be highly sought after in our sailing/racing community. We just had to make sure that we got to ride on at least one of those charters as the owners' representative on board.

"Fortunately, it worked out for both of us and in 1988, six months after my third heart operation (and just a year after the Race For Life) I was aboard Swiftsure for the Pacific Cup, a highly regarded race between San Francisco and Hawaii.

"We had chartered the boat to a group of doctors. In addition to George and I, my son Joe was aboard for his second sail to Hawaii. He was fifteen years old and this time his trip was going to be quite a bit shorter than our seventeen-day family trip.

Saturday June 16th is the day
The *Virgilio Crew* will give Mom & Dad away

After *25 years* they couldn't be hotter
The anniversary couple will *"do it again"* on the water

With family & friends gathered on *the bow*
We want you to join us for cocktails and *"The Vow"*

So meet us at the *Kona Kai Club Quay*
Where at *6p.m. sharp* we'll cruise down the bay!

RSVP 222-9963   Casual boating attire

Dick and Bea's 25th wedding anniversary, 1990.

"Well, as I had hoped, the thrill of sailing twenty-five knots downwind was fantastic. To do it with my son by my side was truly priceless. Through all of this Bea was having a hard time understanding my passion for adventure and was extremely happy when, after this trip, I was able to sell my half of the boat and return to being a one-boat sailor.

"In the summers of 1989, 1991, and 1995, I found myself once again on the Pacific, heading west to Hawaii on our family boat Bravo, and with different combinations of my children. My daughter Christiana was with me on two of the crossings, which gave her three crossing in four years. Bea and I were not surprised therefore when, after graduation from UCLA in 1991, that she pursued a career in yachting."

Dick and Christiana aboard Bravo, *sailing to Hawaii, 1991.*

In addition to Christiana, son Joe and daughter Gina were aboard for the Hawaii cruises. Bea and the other children, when available, would meet them in Hilo, and they would spend a month or so cruising the waters of Hawaii. Today, Christiana is a highly regarded captain of a 172-foot motor yacht that travels the globe.

"Christiana's first job on a yacht was as a deck hand on a 105-foot sailboat named Cinderella II. In 1993, she was able to get me a ride during a trans-Atlantic crossing from the Caribbean to England. When she asked me if I was interested, my response was probably pretty darned predicable. I sat bolt upright and said 'yes' as fast, as loud, and as convincingly as I knew how.

"Consequently, I was able to enjoy my first Atlantic crossing with her, and in a sailboat. Since that time we have enjoyed no fewer than fifteen crossings in the motor yacht that she is now skipper of—Big Eagle.

"During this ten-year period, Bea and I also enjoyed multiple trips to British Columbia and Alaska in a friend's sixty-five-foot power boat. In addition, I participated in multiple sailing races to Man-

Dick and daughter Christiana crossing the Atlantic in sailing vessel Cinderella, *1994.*

zanillo, Puerto Vallarta, and Cabo San Lucas.

"When I wasn't racing, Bea and I were aboard a variety of escort yachts for these Mexican races. Even though the children were getting older and pursuing their own interests, we still managed to get in several weeks of family skiing every winter.

Christiana.

"All five of our children graduated from college between 1988 and 1998, and our oldest two daughters, Maria and Angela, got married in 1992 and 1993, making the possibility of early retirement not just a dream but a reality.

"I continued to progress up the ladder on the board of directors at the San Diego Yacht Club, becoming commodore in 1997. With my responsibilities and time commitments here in San Diego vastly minimized, I was getting close to attacking another item on my bucket list—sailing the South Pacific in my own boat—which we eventually did.

Boat Prep? $10,000. Supplies? $5,000. Celebrating the 4th of July mid-Pacific on the way to Hawaii with your kids? PRICELESS (1994).

"There's something about the challenge, about being in that big ocean on a little piece of equipment. You're up against all that water and the elements. It takes a lot of responsibility, and it's certainly a huge challenge, but the reward is the excitement and the sense of accomplishment when you're done.

"When I did it by myself, it was the biggest challenge because I was all alone. When I did it with my family, it was still a challenge, but it was different. It gave me a chance to sit back and talk with my

Dick with Captain Christiana and good friend Bob Spriggs aboard Big Eagle *after an Atlantic crossing from Malta, 2010.*

family, my children. It gave me a unique opportunity to learn from my children, and learn I did.

"That's the reason I'm still doing it at eighty years of age. I no longer do long sailing voyages, but I frequently make passages with my daughter Christiana on Big Eagle. I get to spend quality time with her, but I'm also challenged at sea with things like navigation and planning. It makes me realize there is no room for senility in my life. In a way, it's a test for me, and I love every minute of it.

"In the past fifteen years, I have traveled more than 120,000 miles on her yacht, including seventeen trans-Atlantic crossings. I've transited the Panama Canal four times and have cruised to ports from St. Petersburg, Russia to Juneau, Alaska. I've taken the boat to the Eastern Mediterranean, the western Great Lakes, and visited many, many exotic ports, including Casablanca.

"I'm so very grateful to Christiana for giving me the opportunity to continue to enjoy the challenges of the sea as I've grown older."

Over the course of months of interviewing and remembering,

laughing at his mistakes and beaming over his successes, Dick admitted that extended sea voyages push him physically, mentally, and spiritually like nothing he had ever experienced. He described how he rides the edge against opponents that are just so much bigger — the ocean, the wind, the elements—and he smiles when reminiscing about that incredible feeling he gets when he reaches his destination.

"Victory. I suppose that's the best word to describe it. I've conquered many things, not the least of which are my own mind and body. I rest up, and then I want to do it again, and again, and again; not because I long to visit a particular country or port, but simply because, after all I've been through, I do this because I can."

Aboard Big Eagle, with his daughter Christiana, Dick has visited such ports-of-call in Italy, France, Costa Rica, Panama, Morocco, Nassau, St. Martin, Spain, Puerto Rica, Russia, Scotland, Canada, Mexico—Cabo San Lucas and La Paz—as well as Alaska and numerous ports throughout the greater United States.

At last check, in addition to the 125,000 miles logged aboard Big Eagle with Christiana, Dick has logged an additional 75,000 miles on other boats, both under sail and power.

And those numbers continue to grow . . .

Dick and Christiana on Big Eagle. *Panama Canal, 2008.*

222

EIGHTEEN

South Pacific

That darned Bucket List. It's hard to say after all these years if it was a blessing or a curse. One thing's for certain, the lure of Jeff Chandler's South Pacific remained on Dick's Bucket List, and he was determined to check it off.

"I know it must sound silly for a grown man to keep adding items to his bucket list, but you have to remember, I started late on all these adventures. And, yes, I did have one more thing I wanted to do before I died. I wanted to sail the South Pacific.

"My son Joe was graduating from the University of San Diego. It was 1996 and he was 23. He didn't have any real plans about what he wanted to do, and I saw an opportunity to fulfill my dream as well as give him some time to get his act together and figure out what he wanted to do in life.

"I was excited about doing such a trip with just the two of us, and felt if nothing else, such an adventure might give him some responsibility and serve as a good stepping stone for his future.

"I asked him how much money he had. He had inherited more than $15,000 from his grandfather. I said, 'I'll tell you what. Here's the plan. I want us to do the South Pacific together. When we get there, we can charter the boat and make a little money to pay our way as we go. But I'm going to need a full-time captain, so I can come back and forth for a while, finishing things up stateside.'

"I was, at that time, getting ready to retire, and my term as commodore of San Diego Yacht Club was coming to a close. As my responsibilities in San Diego became less and less, I hoped to spend more time with Joe on the boat.

"I suggested Joe put up some money as equity in the boat. I wasn't going to make this a gift. But whatever we made chartering the boat we would share.

"One of the other benefits for him was that he could surf all those exotic and tropical breaks he always wanted to surf. He was very excited at the plan and agreed.

"Preparing the boat meant getting a dive compressor for it. That year, 1996, we departed the yacht club and sailed directly for Tahiti. I had about a month to make that passage and get the boat situated.

"What a wonderful experience that was with Joe. We crossed the equator together and wound up in the Marquesas Islands. Then we sailed to Papeete. From there I came home, and Joe stayed in the Society Islands, exploring Bora Bora, Moorea, and all those special island locales we had always heard about, read about, and dreamed about.

Sailing proved to be the great common denominator.

"We did three charters there—people from San Diego. Joe made some money and got good tips; the boat made some money. Meanwhile, Bea and I were doing our thing back here, moving and going through our transitional thing.

"Once I wrapped up loose ends in San Diego, I flew to Tonga to meet Joe and the boat. We set course immediately for Fiji. It was hurricane season, so we chose to hang out in Fiji for six months. Bea joined us and we had a great time there. Joe, meanwhile, found a job at Namotua, one of the surf islands near Tavarua.

"I got restless after a time and flew back to the States. I took some good friends down, and they chartered the boat. Spending ten days or two weeks on the boat was perfect for me as we cruised around Fiji

Bravo *at anchor in Bora Bora.*

and surrounding waters, with Joe in charge of the boat and doing a great job of that. My ultimate goal was Australia."

During this time, Dick and his son continued to grow closer. They had sailed to Hawaii on Bravo twice, but this trip was bountiful, not just for Dick's relationship with his son, but with all of his children. Sailing proved to be the great common denominator — the glue — that helped make the Virgilio family special.

"Yeah, it was phenomenal spending quality time with my son in Tahiti. How many fathers have a chance to spend a month on a forty-six-foot boat with one of their kids? You're either gonna end up hating each other or loving each other. Fortunately for us, it was the latter.

"I never had that sort of experience with my own father — never anything even close. Granted, I have had the most amazing adventures with each and every one of my children, but this was very special. Joe and I were definitely closer after this adventure.

"Of course, we had our ups and downs. I mean, he got really upset at me at times. For example, originally we were going to go

Dick and son Joe leaving San Diego, crossing the equator, and approaching Huka Hiva in the Marquesas.

around the world, but then he fell in love with this girl he met in Fiji. She was from Perth. So the minute we got anywhere near Australia, he was gone. But, you know what? That turned out all right also.

During this voyage, Dick and Joe went from Fiji to New Caledonia, then over to the Great Barrier Reef and Hamilton Island. At that point Bea flew over and joined them on Hamilton Island, which lies northeast of Australia, along the Great Barrier Reef.

"We were looking forward to sailing down to Sydney, which is about 1,200 miles from the Great Barrier Reef—a fair bit of distance. At that point, Joe informed us he was going to Perth to meet his girlfriend and spend some time there. So Bea and I elected to do the trip alone, just the two of us.

"It took us about ten days and the weather was pretty rough. The Australian coast guard were very good. They kept us safe and wouldn't let us leave the harbor if it was coming on a blow. Still, it

Dick with son Joe, somewhere in the Society Islands, 1997.

was pretty stressful for Bea. Thinking back, it was stressful for me, too, because I knew that if I had a heart attack, or my defibrillator went off, or something else happened to incapacitate me, that Bea wouldn't have been able to handle the boat alone.

"Well, we finally reached Sydney. I realized then that Joe wasn't going to come back and finish our around-the-world deal. I had done what I wanted to do, which was to see the South Pacific islands. I didn't find Jeff Chandler, but I thought about him all the time.

"And yet, there we were, Bea and I, alone on Bravo. I realized then that my kids were practically all gone. They had their own lives, and this was no longer going to be our family boat. We had become so absorbed in our family life and our many adventures that it just sort of sneaked up on us — the empty nester syndrome."

Bea and Dick remained in Sydney for about two months. They saw the New Year in, then made arrangements to have Bravo brought

Dick and Christiana, 1994, off Pico Island in the Azores, aboard the sailing yacht Cinderella *making a delivery to England. They were both on board as deckhands.*

back by freighter. They had done San Francisco and Tinsley Island; they had sailed her to Catalina Island 25 times; they had done four trips to Hawaii and now the South Pacific. If ever there was a well-traveled and happy boat, this was it.

"I really didn't want to bring the boat back, except I didn't know what else to do with it. And I certainly wasn't going to sail it back.

"Bea and I talked about it and decided it probably wasn't the best idea to continue such sailing adventures at my age, and with a heart that I really couldn't trust. So, we came to accept the fact that we were now in our sixties, that my medical condition was a reality, and that to continue with this lifestyle wasn't the most sensible thing to do."

***Man, but that boat had
Seen a lot of sea miles.***

Dick and Christiana, 2010, 16 years later, off Pico Island aboard Big Eagle, *on a delivery from Italy to Boston. Dick is still a deckhand but Christiana is now the captain.*

Just as Dick finalized arrangements to bring the boat back on the freighter, he and Bea were sitting at the Pitwater Yacht Club in their slip, and some guy comes along and asks if Bravo was a Kelly Peterson 46. Dick yelled back, "Yeah." They guy asked Dick if he would consider selling it.

"Well, you know what my answer was. I signed a deal with him right then and there. And we saved $25,000 in freighter fees to boot.

They flew home, and a couple of years later Joe returned home.

"Looking back, it was a great experience for us as a family. As for Bravo, the new owner had big plans, but his wife could only cruise with him for about two months. So they sold it in Indonesia to a guy who sailed her to Seattle and outfitted her for the Pacific Northwest.

"The last I saw of old Bravo was down in Puerto Vallarta. Man, but that boat had seen a lot of sea miles, a lot of miles."

✳✳✳

Family gathered on the stern of Bravo.

All this time, in the back of his mind, was Dick's practice and a gnawing desire to retire from medicine.

"The kids were all gone off to grow their own lives by then. As I mentioned earlier, all of my five children had graduated from college. My two oldest were married, and the days of tuition and helping out were behind us.

1996 was a real turning point in Dick's life. He had retired from medicine before the South Pacific trip, but still helped out with surgeries. For 35 years he had worked very hard in his job. He would have liked to retire earlier, but couldn't—not until he was sure the kids were headed down a good road.

"Towards the end of my medical career, I was besieged with heart issues, and I no longer had the enthusiasm for what I was doing. If

View from Dick's living room of Big Eagle, *arriving in San Diego.*

you can't be enthusiastic about it, you shouldn't be doing it because, in the end, you're just not performing up to your standards as a surgeon.

"When it becomes a drudgery to go into the hospital, into your office, to see patients—well, then it's time to think about moving on. I always took my work extremely serious. If you don't have that passion any longer, you shouldn't apologize for that; you should just accept that you did your best and move on. No regrets.

"Those thirty-five years took their toll on me, that's for sure, but I'm proud of my career and, after all, I was fortunate enough to survive it all and at that point I just wanted to enjoy not having that pressure on me any longer.

"Near the end, things began to upset me. One episode in particular really sunk in and left an impression. One day a police officer was brought in with a gunshot wound to the chest.

"We worked on him and worked on him. His partner was in the operating room with us. We did all we could but couldn't save him.

It was a brutal moment to look up and have to tell his buddy he had died.

"An hour later they brought in the perpetrator—the man who shot the officer I had just unsuccessfully worked on. This fellow also had a terrible gunshot wound. Wouldn't you know it? He survived.

"It was right about then I began asking myself what the hell I was doing. I mean, why was I even working on that scumbag? It was a sign that it was time for me to get the hell out.

Well, Jesus, I didn't save everybody.

"Also during this time frame, I operated on two close friends. One was my dear friend's daughter, who had died. The other was a son of a very good friend of ours, who was critically injured in a surfing accident. I operated on him four or five times after his accident. We couldn't save him.

"Of course, throughout the surgeries my own kids would look at me and say, 'What are you worried about Dad? You're going to save him. You save everybody.'

"Well, Jesus, I didn't save everybody. And then I had to come home and tell the kids their friend Timmy had died.

"The kid died in ICU at Mercy Hospital, with my hand in his chest and blood all over me. I couldn't even tell his mother right away. All I could think about was taking a shower in the doctors' lounge. It wasn't just the blood I was washing off; it was a lot of things that had been building up in my brain, culminating with this death.

"That was the beginning of the end for my medical career. I began to doubt what I was doing and I just didn't want to do this anymore. I never wanted to work on another criminal, drug runner, or someone who was doing harm to people. The trouble is, as a doctor, your job is to save people—all people, even the criminals.

"I walked out of Mercy Hospital and never looked back. I told my friends that if they ever saw me at that hospital again—unless I was visiting a former colleague or patient—to shoot me.

"Other doctors had trouble walking away. They would use every opportunity to visit the hospital—conferences, free coffee and donuts. Not me.

"I never ever once picked up a medical book after that. Or thought about my life as a doctor, or missed it. People would ask me how retirement was going and I'd say, well, I haven't flunked yet. There was never a better time to retire, and I've never looked back.

"Nowadays, the only medical consultation I do is with close friends and family. I do it for people as an advocate, not as a hands-on do-something kind of guy. You gotta pick the people; I mean I still do it, still stay in touch with the medical world from afar. For example, I knew who to call if I needed to know the name of a good XYZ doctor. Even though I didn't know that particular doctor because he was coming along when I left.

"You see, I had other things I wanted to do. I wanted to spend time with my family. I wanted to ski. I wanted to sail the South Pacific, because, in all honesty, I never expected to still be here at the age of eighty.

"Looking back now, I don't think even Bea understood why I retired. I don't think she or the children could ever understand what I was going through at the time—my heart condition, the workload, saving the bad guys and watching the good ones die.

"I left a lot of money on the table when I retired. I had sold my practice, sold the trauma contract, and just walked away. I hope my children understand why I quit, and I hope that they understand it was the right thing to do. When I think of all I've accomplished, and all I've done since my retirement, it's staggering. I don't mean just the sailing adventures. We've done so very, very much together as a family. It's wonderful how many opportunities we've created as a family.

"Those last five or six years in practice were tough—extremely depressing. Whether it was by my own hands, somebody else's hands, or by God's hands. It was time for me to get out.

"And yet, even to this day I feel my family deserves an explanation.

And that's why I'm writing this book. Maybe when they read this they'll get it; they'll understand the reasons dad stopped helping people. Like I said at thirty-six, when I had my first heart operation, there was nobody who could be the father to my children, or a husband to Bea, except me. I wanted to see my grandchildren grow up. I wanted to be there with them. I wanted to have a

Dick's good friend Nick Frazee, who passed while this book was being written. "I miss you, Nick, and thanks for being such a role model for all of your friends who, like you, were husbands and fathers."

relationship with my family that I never had with my father or brother. Thank the Lord I've been blessed to be able to have that.

"They say you don't measure the success of a man by how much money he has, or by his status and business. My dear friend Nick Frazee died recently. I saw first-hand the wonderful relationship he had with his children, and they with him, as they gathered to his side near the end.

"Nick was as successful as one man could be in business. But his success in his own family interactions was even greater. And that's what I'd like to be known for. I don't want people looking at my win/loss record in the surgical theatre, or how much money I made. I want them to know how much I love my family, and they me."

EPILOGUE

To My Family

This final chapter, this epilogue of my life history, should be the easiest to write but in many ways it is turning out to be the most difficult. It's not that I don't know what I want to say to my wife and children; it's because I am afraid that I will leave something important out and not realize it until after the book is written.

At the same time, I don't want to sound morbid, but there is so much I want to say to my wonderful family, and once I'm gone, I won't have the chance to do that.

Bea

I need to start by talking to my beautiful wife, Bea, who has been married to me for the last 52 years and together with me for 55 years. I still remember first meeting you on the steps of the BOQ at the Bethesda Naval Hospital.

You were a recent graduate of nursing school and a recently commissioned Lt. JG in the Navy. I had just finished my first year of medical school and was an ensign in the navy. When I first laid eyes on you I said to myself, "Self I want to marry that girl." In spite of my youthful bravado, I was scared to death to even say hello.

Fortunately, my roommate, Dan White, was not socially shy like I

Renewal of vows at 50th wedding anniversary officiated by good friend Father Quinn.

was and within several minutes he had convinced you and your room-mate to go out with us.

That was the good news. The bad news was that he grabbed you up and left me with your roommate. Of course, I drove and spent the rest of the night looking through the rearview mirror at him trying to make out, with you calling him every name in the book. With time I finally got up enough nerve to ask you out and the rest is history.

To be honest, I never thought there was a snowball's chance in hell that you would actually go out with me. By the time I went back to medical school in the fall, I was so in love with you that I had a hard time concentrating on my studies.

My mind was constantly preoccupied with thoughts of you. You were everything that I could have hoped for in a friend and a wife. You were absolutely gorgeous, had a personality that was off the charts, a smile that made me melt. Most importantly, you were Italian.

You were too good to be true, and I was scared to death to ask you to marry me because I was sure that you would say no. I wasn't what you would call handsome, I had a terrible temper, was impatient, and

50th wedding anniversary cake cutting.

my family was as dysfunctional as any could get. I didn't even have any money, as you will recall from having to pay for our dinners and movies.

The reason that it took me so long to propose to you was because of my fear of rejection. My God, I would have asked you after our first date if I had had any confidence in myself. Finally, the Royers told me that if I didn't ask you to marry me, and soon, that someone else would.

So, after two years of dating I got the nerve to propose. When you said yes I couldn't believe it, and all I could do was cry. Bea, that day you made me the happiest man in the world. Waiting until our wedding night to consummate our relationship made my love and respect for you that much greater.

I guess it's a good thing we did because our first born, a beautiful girl, Maria was born exactly nine months to the day after our wedding. I know that your mother was probably counting down to the hour.

Suddenly we were parents. Watching you effortlessly transform into motherhood was truly amazing. I said to myself, "Self, we have to

50th anniversary dinner.

have more children so they can experience what having a great mother is all about." I don't think I was actually thinking four in the next seven years, but every one of our children has been a Blessing from God.

Thank you, my darling, from the bottom of my heart, for being such a wonderful, loving, and understanding mother to our five children over the last half century.

During those 52 years of marriage we have had smooth and rough seas, both on and off the water.

I will never forget our first storm that occurred just three months after Maria was born. I volunteered to go to the Naval Hospital in Da Nang, Vietnam, for a 13-month tour of duty. I had this compulsion to do my part in helping our young men, who were getting injured in that very unpopular war.

I am sure that knowing I volunteered, and was not ordered to go to Vietnam, made it even harder for you. I tried to explain my decision at that time (and I've devoted a portion of the book to this), but at the time, I'm sure none of it made any sense to you.

238

Dick and Bea, with good friends Bob and Joanne Royer (and Skipper), at 50th.

I hope that you understood at the time, and have come to peace with it all these years later. I wasn't running away from you and Maria; rather, I was doing my little part to try to make things better for the sons of many, many other mothers.

My life has been full of difficult decisions, but leaving you and Maria that morning at Dulles Airport, in Washington, and knowing that I would not be back for a very long 13 months, has to top the list. I was confident then that you were strong enough to weather the storm. I could only hope that I was going to be as strong in the many challenges and adventures that awaited me.

Of course, you had to up the difficulty scale by having our second daughter, Angela, three months before I returned. Who was that doctor who told us that you couldn't get pregnant if you were still breastfeeding?

There is no doubt that we both finished the year a little stronger than when we started. It made us better able to handle some of the more difficult storms we would encounter over the next 52 years.

So we started our life together by having two children within a year and being separated for 13 months. With that kind of a start did either of us doubt that our life together would be anything but exciting—full of surprises, with highs and lows, good times and bad?

The next seven years saw three more children born, mixed in with a new job, a move to California, and, of course my first heart attack and bypass operation. The only surprise for me is that I am still alive at age 80 to tell you how much I love and admire you, Bea. Through all of this chaos, you remained strong, reassuring me, and the children, that all was going to be OK.

I will never forget leaving the ICU for my first open-heart surgery. You had the four children clinging to you, and Gina was rolling around in your belly, due to come out in just a week.

You squeezed my hand while kissing me and said to all of us, "Don't worry, Daddy is going to be fine."

I don't know whether you believed it or not, but your confidence and strength was reassuring not only to me, but I am sure to the children as well.

You would be tested over and over again as time went on and we were challenged with various setbacks. The children and I could always count on you being strong and holding us together as a family. I could not have hoped for a better soul mate, friend, lover, and mother to our children when I first met you on those BOQ steps all those years ago.

You always seemed to know when I really needed your support, and not your scorn. You would always wait until the crises was over to present the latter. No time was that more evident than when we broke down on the way to Hawaii, and I was sure we were going to be lost at sea.

I tried to present a confident attitude to the children, but you knew how much I was hurting. At night, when I would break down and cry, you would comfort me and tell me that we were going to get through this ordeal.

It wasn't until we were safe in Hilo that you uttered the words, "Virgilio, you dumb shit." Thank you for being so sensitive to my feelings all those years.

As time went on I was certain there would come a morning where I simply wouldn't wake up. Still, I continued to fanaticize that I would live to celebrate our 50th wedding anniversary.

I don't know why this milestone was so important to me, but it was. Our children made it a weeklong event that became an unbelievably real tribute to our life together. Everyone at the dinner had something special to say about us, and it was a truly beautiful event. I was so taken up in the moment that the dinner was over and I had forgotten to give my speech about how wonderful our 50 years had been, and how my admiration for you had no end.

The moment I realized my screw-up, I couldn't believe it. I felt like a real idiot for weeks thereafter, and I'm so relieved that I have this opportunity to let you and the rest of the family know how very much you mean to me.

Thank you, Bea, for putting up with me all these years, and for being such a beautiful and loving wife, mother, and grandmother. You are truly the greatest woman on the planet.

My Children

Maria, Angela, Christiana, Joe, and Gina—you guys and your children, without a doubt, are the magnificent legacy that Mom and I will leave when we move on and join the Lord in Heaven.

I am going to speak to you collectively, and at times individually, depending on how my fragmented thoughts rise to the surface.

As you read the early chapters of my book, you will realize that my relationship with my father was less than ideal, and I address that at the end of this epilogue. When Mom became pregnant with Maria, I was scared to death that maybe being a dysfunctional father was a genetic thing.

I did not have a clue as to how I would eventually be graded on

Dick, Bea and their five children at the 50th wedding anniversary.

my fatherhood skills. I knew nothing going in, except that I didn't want to be like my father was to me. I always say I didn't know how to be a good father, but I knew I didn't want to be a bad one, and that bad example, my own father, was all I had to go by for benchmarks.

I just knew that I wanted to love my children to death, to be there when they needed me, and stay out of the way when I wasn't needed.

Having made just about every mistake possible in my own youth, I knew that each of you would have your share of missteps along the way. I tried hard to be supportive during those times and not judgmental.

I wanted you to learn from your mistakes and move on. What you didn't need was someone like me berating you, making you feel guilty, and crushing your ego. I grew up in that kind of environment, and I knew how traumatic it was for me.

Family Portrait at Dick and Bea's 50th wedding anniversary.

When I look at all of you now, as mature adults, I feel that both Mom and I must have done some things correctly with our parenting skills. Of course you guys will be the final judge of that.

When I observe the growth of our nine grandchildren, there is little doubt that you guys have improved on our program. I could not be more proud of the legacy that Mom and I will leave when we move on.

Maria, leaving you and Mom when you were just three months old was one of the hardest decisions I ever had to make. I hope after reading the early part of this book that you understand what was going through my mind at the time.

I was not running away from you and Mom, but was motivated by a sense of duty to country. I took being a doctor very seriously and wanted to be available to help those young men in that faraway war.

They say, "Courage is being scared to death but still going out to meet the challenge." I was scared to death the entire year I was gone, but I came home a better person. For my efforts, I returned to a home

The Virgilio clan celebrating Dick's 80th birthday. Puerto Vallarta, Mexico. 2017.

with a beautiful wife and two beautiful baby girls. I was about to start a career as a father and, you talk about being scared, but I knew that I had courage and was anxious to get started on my voyage of raising a family.

I know that I have made mistakes along the way, but I hope that you, your sisters, and brother know that my love and respect for you guys has no end—no boundaries.

It wasn't until I developed my heart problems in 1974 that I came to realize how screwed up my priorities were, and that I was probably on the wrong tract to becoming a good father and husband. You guys were eight, seven, five, and three years old. Gina was two weeks away from being born. I was 36 years old, going into heart surgery to correct blockage of my coronary arteries.

Bypass surgery was in its infancy, and I was frightened—oh so frightened—that I was going to die in the surgery and not have the opportunity to see you guys grow up and become adults.

I was sure that Gina was being sent to replace me in our family. As I was being taken down to the operating room, I remember looking at you kids and Mom and realizing for the first time in my adult life that the only thing that made me unique was not that I could cut and sew and occasionally save a life; there were a lot of doctors who could do that; but I was the only one who could be the father to my children and the husband to your mom.

It was at that moment that I said to myself, "Self, if you are lucky enough to survive this surgery, you are going to change your priorities in life." It would be family first and everything, including medicine, would have to get in line behind you guys.

As the years went on and you kids were maturing into adulthood, I am sure that at times the "family first" thing got to be a real pain in the ass. I would drag you guys and Mom on one crazy adventure after another, including a voyage across the Pacific.

I just wanted us to be together, and for you guys to have some memories of us doing things as a family. I had none of those memories from my childhood, and it continues to be a dark spot in my memory, and in my life.

I hope that I was able to leave you with some good memories and stories to share with your family and friends. If not, I am sorry for putting you through those crazy times, but please always remember that my intentions were good.

You have all matured into beautiful people, and made Mom and me extremely proud. You each have a unique personality that makes it hard to believe that you are from the same gene pool, and grew up in the same environment. Please believe me when I tell you that there were no favorites when it came to you kids.

You each brought something special into my life and are the reason that I am still around at age 80. Where do you think I got the strength to fight my various medical problems? From you!

There were times that I just wanted to give up the fight and sail into the sunset, but my love and respect for each of you, your families, and Mom has continued over the years to give me the strength to do whatever it takes to stay alive.

If that meant another heart operation, a defibrillator change, or some experimental hepatitis C therapy, so be it. I am one of the lucky guys who had a reason to stay alive, and my family and the Lord above have gifted that reason to me.

I thank each of you for being who and what you are, and for giving me a purpose for fighting to stay alive a little longer. When I do leave you, please always remember how proud I am to have left you and your children as my legacy.

You have given me more joy and happiness than I could have ever hoped for, and now, finally, after seven decades, I have those family memories that were so conspicuously missing from my own childhood.

My Grandchildren

Alex, Charlie, Nicole, Joey, Jack, Kannan, Kayla, Olivia, and Matilda, what a lineup of beautiful people. You guys will never know how much happiness and joy you have brought into my life, and of course into Gammy's as well.

As you all get older and more independent, we see less of you, but our love and respect for each and every one of you is embedded in our hearts. We think of you constantly.

I hope reading this book will give you a better understanding of who your granddad really was and why family meant so much to him. There are a few important lessons that can be gleamed from this sometimes boring book, and I hope that as each of you mature into young adults you will be able to identify and learn from them. You younger kids will probably have to find the book and dust it off, but one day I think you'll agree it was worth the effort.

You guys are extremely fortunate to have such wonderful parents who not only love you with all their heart and soul, but who are, yes, believe it or not, understanding of how hard it is to grow up in this crazy world we live in.

Their love for you has no end, and they will always be there for you when you need help the most. Remember, no matter how bad you think you screwed up, your mom and dad will be there for support

Dick and Bea with their nine grandchildren in front of their house, 2015.

and guidance to help you. You have no better friends than your family, so when you need help, turn to them first and foremost.

You are indeed blessed to have so much great support. Your "team" is made up not just by your parents, but also from your aunts, uncles, and cousins, and, yes, even your siblings.

Trust me, Joey and Jack, it won't be long before you guys are the best of friends. I predict you will have each other's backs throughout your long and interesting lives. I just wish I had had a brother who cared enough about me to fight with me when I was growing up. Had that been the case, I know I would have had a friend to count on throughout the years.

Gammy and I feel blessed that we were able to take the two Disney cruises with you guys. I have never been more proud to be a granddad than during the time we spent with you on the ship. You never gave me any reason to be upset with your behavior. I can't tell you how many of the passengers would come up and tell me what

Grandkids at Dick's 80th birthday celebration. Puerto Vallarta, Mexico. 2017.

Dick starting his granddaughter early on the water.

a beautiful and well-behaved family we had. Gammy and I will never forget the quality time we had to spend with you. Thank you so much for making us so proud to be your grandparents.

I suppose you must wonder why the title of my life history is *Strong In, Strong Out*. I'll touch on it here, but I hope you'll still read the book.

It's one of the lessons I have learned over the years in dealing with my personal crises, both physical and mental. If I was strong and positive going into the crisis, I would

Dick at home with his best friend Skipper.

be strong when it was over. I saw too many individuals give up on life after a setback. The thing they all had in common was that they were weak and negative going into the crisis. So please remember as you deal with your own setbacks in life to approach them with a strong and positive attitude.

Ode To My Father

As you've read throughout this book, I had no relationship with my father. I even ran away from home to escape him. Later in life, we simply avoided each other.

When my mother died suddenly in 1984, my father was understandably upset and very emotional. I remember thinking at the time that it was probably because he knew he would no longer have someone around to take care of his every need, to wait on him hand and foot.

I couldn't wrap my head around any possibility that he might feel the pain of losing someone that he really, truly loved.

At her funeral my father hugged me for the first time that I could ever remember, even though he could never bring himself to say, "I love you, son"; words I longed to hear; words every son needs to hear.

That hug was the only sign of affection I ever remember receiving from my father. And yet, it made me feel even more bitter towards him. Needless to say, I was not overly impressed with the gesture, and for the next several years nothing changed in our icy relationship.

However, as my children grew, it nagged at me. I really wanted my own children to have a relationship with their grandfather, and, hopefully, come away with a few fond memories.

So I decided to make a good-faith gesture to improve my relationship with him. He was my father, after all, and as I got older I began to understand why he had such a hard time showing any affection for his family.

He grew up in an Italian immigrant household where outward demonstrations of love and affection simply did not exist—old country, old school.

In addition to craving some sort of relationship between my children and their grandfather, I didn't want to wake up one day and have him gone, and me feeling guilty that I wasn't there for him in the end. I guess that sums up the difference between us.

More importantly, I didn't want my children to think I had abandoned him when times got rough—when he was old, dying, and all alone. Sadly, my brother, who lived just 200 miles from him, never went to see him and didn't even attend his funeral.

It was not an easy task, but I began to spend a lot of time in Florida, away from my own family, taking care of a man who had never demonstrated any love for me.

As he slept, I found myself staring at him as memories raced through my mind. In the end, there were not many answers to my lifelong questions about my father, but I think I did the right thing by being there by his side. I know my mother would have wanted that.

I can admit now that when he died I was more relieved than sad. Whatever emotional sacrifices I may have made there in the end were worth it. That wouldn't have been the case, had I not swallowed my pride and committed to being there for him in the end.

I have friends who never reconciled with a relative and they all, to a person, were left with deep feelings of guilt when that person passed away.

The good news is that by changing my attitude towards my father, my children were able to spend some quality time with their paternal grandfather and actually come away with fond memories of him.

I think back now and realize that, while my mother was alive, he was jealous of the children and all the time she spent with them. Consequently, he would avoid any prolonged encounters with the family.

I just wish that my mother could have had more quality time with her grandchildren, whom she loved so dearly. Looking back, I think my children are very fortunate to have had so much family in their lives. They will appreciate that more and more the older they become, and as they raise their own children.

In Summary

As we wrap up two years of trying to capture my life between two book covers, I am pleased to turn it over to you, my family, my legacy.

To all my family and friends, I would just say, "When I'm gone, miss me, but let me go."

I love you dearly.

Dick Virgilio

CPSIA information can be obtained
at www.ICGtesting.com
Printed in the USA
BVHW010816221221
624683BV00011B/67/J